magnetic service

Also by Chip R. Bell

Customer Love: Attracting and Keeping Customers for Life
Managers As Mentors: Building Partnerships for Learning
Customers As Partners: Building Relationships That Last
Influencing: Marketing the Ideas That Matter

with Ron Zemke
Service Magic: How to Amaze Your Customers
Knock Your Socks Off Service Recovery
Managing Knock Your Socks Off Service
Service Wisdom: Creating and Maintaining the Customer Service Edge

with Ray Bard, Leslie Stephen, and Linda Webster
The Trainer's Professional Development Handbook

with Oren Harari
Beep Beep!: Competing in the Age of the Road Runner

with Fredric Margolis
Understanding Training: Perspectives and Practices
Instructing for Results: Managing the Learning Process

with Leonard Nadler
Clients and Consultants
The Client-Consultant Handbook

with Heather Shea
Dance Lessons: Six Steps to Great Partnerships in Business and Life

Chip R. Bell and Bilijack R. Bell

magnetic service

secrets for creating passionately devoted customers

BERRETT-KOEHLER PUBLISHERS, INC.
San Francisco

Berrett-Koehler Publishers, Inc.
235 Montgomery Street, Suite 650
San Francisco, CA 94104-2916
Tel: (415) 288-0260 Fax: (415) 362-2512 www.bkconnection.com

Ordering Information
Quantity sales. Special discounts are available on quantity purchases by corporations,
associations, and others. For details, contact the "Special Sales Department" at the
Berrett-Koehler address above.

Individual sales. Berrett-Koehler publications are available through most bookstores.
They can also be ordered direct from Berrett-Koehler: Tel: (800) 929-2929;
Fax: (802) 864-7626; www.bkconnection.com

Orders for college textbook/course adoption use. Please contact
Berrett-Koehler: Tel: (800) 929-2929; Fax: (802) 864-7626.

Orders by U.S. trade bookstores and wholesalers. Please contact
Publishers Group West, 1700 Fourth Street, Berkeley, CA 94710.
Tel: (510) 528-1444; Fax (510) 528-3444.

Berrett-Koehler and the BK logo are registered trademarks of
Berrett-Koehler Publishers, Inc.

Printed in the United States of America

Berrett-Koehler books are printed on long-lasting acid-free paper. When it is available, we
choose paper that has been manufactured by environmentally responsible processes.
These may include using trees grown in sustainable forests, incorporating recycled paper,
minimizing chlorine in bleaching, or recycling the energy produced at the paper mill.

Library of Congress Cataloging-in-Publication Data
Bell, Chip R.
  Magnetic service : the secrets of creating passionately devoted customers /
  Chip R. Bell and Bilijack R. Bell.
    p. cm.
  ISBN 1-57675-236-4
    1. Customer services.   2. Consumer satisfaction.   I. Bell, Bilijack R., 1972–
    II. Title.
HF5415.5B435 2003
658.8′12—dc21   2003043790

FIRST EDITION
07 06 05   10 9 8 7 6 5 4 3

Text design by Detta Penna

Dedicated
to
Nancy Rainey Bell
and
Lisa Dickinson Bell

Contents

Part One
The Secret Side of Magnetic Service

7

Part Two
The Leadership Side of Magnetic Service

89

Contents

Foreword

Another customer service book? Sure, but . . .

It's not your run-of-the-mill, how-to-do-it-better treatise. True, this book is full of great customer service principles, techniques, tips—world-class "secrets" that father-son author team Chip and Bilijack Bell have seen in the hundreds of companies they have worked with and studied. From the front line to finance, from global giant to mom-and-pop, anyone, anywhere can take this book's secrets to heart and apply them right now, right where they are.

At its core, *Magnetic Service* is about what makes someone say, "I'm a Harley guy . . . or woman!" In a way, it's about the power of branding, but not in the usual marketing and advertising sense of the word. It leaves you with a deep understanding of how everything that touches customers affects their loyalty to you.

You will not only hear new twists on familiar customer loyalty themes here like reliability, comfort, listening, and continuous learning. You'll see how today's great service organizations really, really, really know their customers. How they understand that magnetic service is an emotional experience, grounded in honorable values and powered by deep connections between service providers and their customers. How winning customer devotion is not a matter of just delivering *more* value, but *different* value. How magnetic service leadership is a never-ending process, and how leadership comes from every corner of a supportive culture, from people on the front lines and in the back offices who are leaders in everything they do.

So, *Magnetic Service* also talks about stuff like character, honesty, connection, engagement, commitment, trust. If that sounds heady or heavy, don't be put off. Chip and Bilijack use their prodigious gifts of storytelling to show the way regular people live values like these every day in magnetic service organizations. In other words, they show you that this stuff works—and how.

Reading *Magnetic Service* is like going on a ride with America's top customer service icons to learn close up about the excitement, fun, and devotion they experience with their customers. Pick it up today and start riding.

Rich Teerlink
Retired Chairman and CEO
Harley-Davidson, Inc.

Welcome

Welcome! Thank you for exploring magnetic service with us. Customer service is an old and heavily trodden path. One wonders what new could be said about a topic that has spawned a gazillion books. We think there is much more to be learned and shared.

Today's customers are different. Whether we call them customers, clients, patients, guests, members, or citizens, their choices are wider, their requirements more stringent, and their standards more demanding. Those organizations that serve customers well already know that today there is zero tolerance for mediocre performance or poor quality. They also know there is much more of a requirement for not just fairness, but for obvious integrity and trust-producing reliability.

Today's time-crunched customers are also impatient and have little tolerance for organizations that encumber the transaction, often just prior to asking for payment. These are the characteristics of today's marketplace that enticed us to find new guideposts to a more efficient path along an old, familiar trail. If you follow them, you will enter the realm of what we call "magnetic service."

Magnetism 101

We selected "magnetic" to describe the kind of service experience for customers that fosters their enduring passionate devotion because the word has several meanings and thus serves the world of service in several intriguing ways. For example, "magnetic" means having a draw or appeal, as in the case of a person with a "magnetic" personality. In this sense, it is synonymous with "compelling," "alluring," "captivating," and "charismatic."

"Magnetic" also means having the features of a magnet. Its meaning in this sense includes hold, pull, attraction, or inducement.

Magnets on the refrigerator hold pictures and notes. Magnetic service is that service that holds or keeps customers. Magnets exert a steady, utterly reliable pull. The user never has to wonder whether the magnet will perform as it always has—its pull is one of the immutable laws of the universe. Magnetic service should be almost as steadfast. Why? Because when you scrape away all the feature-rich, value-added, clever charm you can use to augment the service experience, customers are left with one core question: Will I get what was promised?

Magnets do not work alone; they only work when they are interacting with something else. Magnetic service is also interactive, not a solitary or "we know what's best for you" thing. Customer devotion is not enhanced by cold, distant consumer research that relies on sterile surveys, statistical objectivity and "box holder" detachment. A magnet—just like service that yields devotion—only works at close range. What is required for the service you provide to have the quality of magnetism?

The subtitle of this book—"Secrets for Creating Passionately Devoted Customers"—also signals that our take on the subject is different from what you might find in the traditional customer loyalty texts. This book is more about the depth of customers' affection than the length of their attraction. Granted, some devoted customers become "customers for life." But we also know that some types of organizations cannot rely on repeat business from the same customer. Growing their business must depend on the word of mouth of passionate advocates. There are also service providers that cannot base their business economics on greater frequency of purchase due to great service. Most people do not purchase big-ticket items like a home or car more often just because the realtor or dealer gave them extraordinary service. Therefore, infatuation with the moment can be as powerful as faithfulness in the future.

Creating Voluntary Cows

This book also goes off the beaten path in that it is, in a way, about branding—a very popular concept these days that has spawned countless books. However, just looking at the origins of branding is, in many ways, more instructive than studying the textbook principles. Branding started as a tool for creating identity. While marking products to identify the maker is as old as time, our most graphic lesson comes from the old West. During the late 1800s, in the western part of the United States where cattle were the primary cash crop, there were no fences to mark territory. Ranch owners needed a device to identify which cattle grazing on the open range belonged to a particular ranch. The act of burning a unique symbol into the hide of a cow became a way to resolve differences over property. Branding was not a ritual elected by the cow, but an identifying mark forced upon it.

Customers are not willing to be treated like property, and they do not like having things forced upon them. They must volunteer their allegiance to a particular "ranch." When you see people labeling themselves as "a Harley guy," or "a Ritz-Carlton traveler," or a "gotta have my Starbucks" person, you are not just witnessing a case of voluntary identification with a motorcycle, hotel, or coffee, but a case of customers sporting the "brand" to which they are devoted. What does it take to provoke this "devotion to the ranch" phenomenon? What would a ranch owner have to do to make the cattle choose the hot tattoo that read "Circle B," instead of the "Lazy L" designating the ranch on the other side of the river? What do world-class magnetic service providers do to brand their connection to their customers?

Branding a connection is very different from branding a commodity. Commodity branding is all about the subtle psychology of packaging and the savvy technology of promotion. It includes careful attention to form, presentation, and value definition. It entails close consideration of trends, fads, and styles. In the world of object branding, the power of peer influence is as compelling as the poetry of ad copy or the charm of a catchy jingle. Watch the ads accompanying the Super Bowl and you'll see commodity branding at its most obvious.

Branding a connection is instead all about focusing on the customer relationship. It is not superior to the branding of an object, it is just fundamentally different. It relies on experience more than image, feeling more than form, and genuineness more than cleverness. Branding a commodity requires knowledge of promotion; branding a connection depends on knowledge of personality. Getting a cow to go freely into the branding pen cannot be achieved with prods and promises but rather through actions that speak perception and trust. So it is with a customer.

In part, this book is about branding your connection with your customers. It examines familiar elements of customer relationships like trust, listening, comfort, and reliability. But it approaches these traits from the back side, so to speak. Trust is not something one gives, but rather something one invites; listening is not about turning a passive ear but rather opening an active, attentive heart. To this important but well-worn mix we have added new components like charisma, curiosity, and character. Customer relationships that will yield to voluntary branding must be elevated to passionate connections; connections that kindle customer devotion must include spirited dealings remembered as remarkable and personal.

Seeing Behind the Curtain

Woven throughout this book is a belief that attracting and keeping a customer's passionate devotion requires a special organizational culture. Customers see the organization through the attitude and practices of the people they encounter. Customer faith in an organization's capacity and desire to support its frontline ambassador is either confirmed or dashed by what that ambassador says and does. While there will always be diligent souls who give magnetic service despite the inadequacies of the organization for which they front, sooner or later the customer gets to see what is behind the curtain, beyond the front guard. And, if that scene fails to match expectations, confidence is eroded and the "shine" quickly wears off the relationship.

The heroes in this book have only one quality in common. Whether corporate president, small business owner, or frontline employee, they exhibit an obvious passion for creating customer experiences that are unforgettable and captivating. They are found in all types and sizes of enterprises. While we will demonstrate a glaring preference for those found in Dallas and Atlanta, we do so only because that is where we live. We also have more examples drawn from the hospitality and retail sectors than any other—again, simply a function of the places where we were able to witness magnetic service up close and personal. And while there is solid and extensive research sitting under the "hood" of this book, it is largely an anecdotally powered tome.

We believe that magnetic service is not limited to any particular region or type of organization. We have seen public servants in highly constricted, bureaucratic settings deliver customer service that would make a five-star hotel green with envy. Our search for the principles and practices we talk about has convinced us that where there is the zeal and courage to serve, magnetic service will emerge; where there is supportive leadership, magnetic service will endure.

We also believe that magnetic service can be learned. And we think this book is a good way to help you get started. Scan it quickly, or read it carefully; read it from front to back, or back to front. How you read it is not important. What matters is that you do something with what you learn. Make a pledge to start with your next customer. Ignore the past, raise your hopes to greater planes, and make it happen. You know that passion is infectious. People smile at you and what do you do? You smile back. A stranger waves and you acknowledge their greeting. Passion is a way of retaliating against a challenging, difficult, and often indifferent world. So go infect someone with your service passion.

Two requests before you do. First, don't save this book. This is not a reference work. You are not going to go back and pull it off the shelf to check a formula, a quote, or a reference. So, give the darn thing away. Pick out the soul you think most needs it and give it to him or her. No fanfare, no cute or caustic note, just simply say, "I liked this book and I thought you would too."

Second, let us know what you think. It was our goal to create a quick read, a "single flight" tome that people could use immediately to start something with their customers. We hope that we have succeeded and that it will make a difference to you and your customers. The last page contains all of the information you need to correspond with us. And we *do* need your feedback.

Chip R. Bell   Bilijack R. Bell
Dallas, Texas   Atlanta, Georgia
                                                    April 2003

Preview

You Don't Know Jack
. . . Or Do You?

Larry is a devoted fan of Jack Daniel's Tennessee Whiskey, but he wasn't always. Sure, he enjoyed it from time to time, along with other brands. Not anymore. If Larry is in a social situation where they don't have Jack, he settles for a glass of club soda. When he hears a friend call for some other brand, he makes a passionate plea for ordering Jack Daniel's instead. How did our friend Larry go from satisfied consumer to passionately devoted customer? And what can his transformation teach us about magnetic service?

"A few years ago," Larry told us one day, "a friend nominated me for membership in the Tennessee Squire Association, kind of a Jack Daniel's fan club. A few weeks later, I received an impressive certificate plus a deed to part of the Jack Daniel Distillery property in Lynchburg, Tennessee. I assumed it was maybe one square inch of land!

"I dismissed it all as a clever marketing ploy," he continued, "until I received a K-1 to include with my income tax return indicating I had a loss of 29 cents due to flood damage on my 'property' in Lynchburg."

Amused, we prodded Larry for more information.

"Well," he continued, "I began to get letters from folks in Lynchburg, like I really was a neighbor. There was one from a fellow who ran the local hardware store wanting to take horse-weed worms from my property to use as fish bait. The county executive of Moore County, Tennessee, wrote requesting an easement across my property so locals could take a shortcut past the distillery to reach Spencer Hole, a popular recreation area. My favorite came from a guy trying to raise a herd of Black Angus cows. He kept getting white-faced calves. When he spotted a white-faced bull on my property, he wrote me for ideas on how to fix the situation."

We were now observing the passion of a wide-eyed groupie at a rock concert. Larry's story continued.

"I'm pretty sure I was a part of the taste test for Gentle-man Jack®, a new brand for Jack Daniel they brought out a few years ago. Before it was on the shelves everywhere, the liquor store owner gave me a taste and wrote down my comments. Jack Daniel Distillery once contacted me and asked me to write my congressman to influence a particular piece of legislation they were trying to get passed. The folks in the local liquor store started asking for my feedback, like they were reps for Jack Daniel. I've gotten calendars, coasters, and catalogs for ordering JD paraphernalia. You want me to keep going?"

We'd heard enough.

What Makes Service Magnetic?

What is it that Jack Daniel Distillery is doing to stir such ardor among customers like Larry? We see several ingredients in our friend's story that are relevant to attracting a customer's passionate devotion.

They Listen ... Really Listen

The Jack Daniel Distillery seems to use the package store owner to solicit feedback ... up close and personal, and without defensiveness.

At least that was Larry's perception. The company sponsors Jack Daniel's Tailgate parties—the JD version of Harley-Davidson's HOG (Harley Owner's Group) gatherings—as a chance for fans of Jack Daniel's to gather for fun and camaraderie. The company communicates the details on their Web site and uses the gathering as a chance to build customer loyalty and gather feedback.

They Value Trust

Log on to www.jackdaniels.com. The first thing you do is type in your birthday to access the site. The first words you read once you enter the Web site say: "Your friends at Jack Daniel's remind you to drink responsibly." The Jack Daniel's online store carries the warning, "This special collection of Jack Daniel's goods is intended for adults of legal drinking age."

The Jack Daniel Distillery knows that trust in the eyes of customers is a moving target—a verb, not a noun—and must be regained and reaffirmed with each new experience. They nourish marketplace trust as carefully as they do the sugar maples used to charcoal filter their whiskey.

They Stir Spirits

Every letter our friend received from the folks in Lynchburg was a creative masterpiece. "I tear it open faster than a check from the IRS," Larry told us, and then added, "I know these letters could be partly fantasy, but they keep me enchanted. Whatever the case, it sure is fun."

No matter what you call it, service with an element of surprise builds customer devotion. That said, magnetic service providers know that you cannot rely on "wowing" the customer as your mainstay . . . at some point you run out of room trying to "one up" the last experience. Still, most of us still enjoy an occasional unexpected gesture or the thrill of knowing that a service moment is unique. Just recall how some surprise you delivered affected an important friend or loved one. Magnetic service providers are masters at striking the right balance.

They Engage Curiosity

Jack Daniel Distillery uses its Web site and mailings to teach customers about everything from "How to sip Jack" to "Recipes with Jack" to "How we actually make Old Number 7." One of their biggest selling items is their collection of Jack Daniel's-inspired cookbooks. "There's a new marinade in their cookbook for barbequed venison," Larry told us. And, before we could stop him, he added, "I even learned recipes for cooking beaver and possum!"

Today's customers seek learning in practically every facet of life. The organization that is able to implant enlightenment into the customer's experience will win customer devotion.

They Foster Inclusion

When Jack Daniel Distillery invited Larry to write to his congressman, they were using inclusion as a strategy for sparking customer devotion. Customers' devotion toward an organization can ratchet up dramatically when they get an opportunity to put some "skin in the game."

Inclusion not only captures the creativity and competence of customers as they serve *with* you, but it inspires their commitment and allegiance, as well. Granted, there are customers who are not interested in participation. And there are times when customer inclusion would not be appropriate. As Jack Daniel Distillery has learned, the secret is knowing when and how to include.

They Value Customer Comfort

How can a product like Jack Daniel's be said to offer comfortable service? Jack Daniel's shows that they know that customers' needs vary. The product comes in every conceivable size—from a "single drink" pony bottle to a half-gallon container. And there are dozens of variations on the theme. Jack Daniel's sells barbeque sauce, lemonade, charcoal, and a host of other products, all flavored with the beloved beverage. Plus their Web site and store displays are accessible, conveying a touch of old-fashioned hospitality.

They Demonstrate Character

Jack Daniel Distillery obviously cares about the quality of their product. They proudly display on the bottle the many awards the Tennessee sipping whiskey has won. They also care about being a quality organization—demonstrating sensitivity to the fact that they are promoting alcohol consumption. They know a quality experience with their products comes with responsibility, and they boldly trumpet that fact. Organizations that are willing to take courageous, principled stands reassure customers that they are dealing with a solid organization likely to stand the test of time.

• • •

Jack Daniel's whiskey might seem like an odd opening exemplar of magnetic service. We are obviously not advocating the irresponsible consumption of spirits. Nor are we on the Jack Daniel's payroll as sales reps, cheerleaders, or stockholders. We just think that Jack Daniel's clearly shows how a product-based company can build brand loyalty and consumer devotion through an eclectic collection of magnetic experiences. If a company in the business of making an object can astound their customers, think of the unlimited potential that organizations in the business of making memories have!

What the Jack Daniel's story demonstrates is that magnetic service is first and foremost bold, imaginative, and stimulating. At Jack Daniel's—and at all the service organizations we explore-magnetic service has a kind of joyful "wake-up call" dimension that makes the customer sit up and take notice. Magnetic service might be daring, or it might not be. It might be "out-loud" assertive, or it might be quietly provocative. It is always unexpected and ends up being a "shining moment" in the memory of the customer. Its power lies in its capacity to stir the emotion of the recipient.

Magnetic service involves a quest for being remarkable in the marketplace. "Remarkable takes originality, passion, guts, and daring," wrote Seth Godin, author of *Purple Cow*. "Not just because going through life with passion and guts beats the alternative (which it does), but because it's the only way to be successful. Today, the one sure way to fail is to be boring. Your one chance for success is to be remarkable."

The path to customer devotion is not complex. But it is by no means easy. Magnetic service begins with treating customers in new ways. If you ground your relationship with them in trust, show that you understand them, touch their spirits, teach them, let them witness your character, and occasionally charm them, they will passionately reward you with their devotion, their advocacy, and their funds.

Part One

The Secret Side of Magnetic Service

. . . . .

There are people who gleefully pay five bucks for a cup of Starbucks coffee, gratefully pay hundreds of dollars to stay at a Ritz-Carlton Hotel, and loyally spend twenty-five grand for a Harley-Davidson motorcycle they wait a long time to get! Where's the logic? Customer devotion jettisons rational economics straight into the stratosphere.

Devotion to Starbucks, Ritz-Carlton, or Harley-Davidson is not about a beverage, hotel, or form of transportation. It's about an experience—an experience as profound and unmistakable as that of a schoolboy smitten for the first time! Granted, the product or outcome must be very good, but not necessarily perfect. Harley devotees grudgingly acknowledge that there really are technologically better bikes. But neither Suzuki nor BMW can match the gratification of a Harley owner on a Sunday afternoon ride with other loyalists. Devotion springs from something else.

Customers who are devoted to your unit or organization act very differently from customers who are simply loyal. Passionately devoted customers not only forgive you when you err, they help you correct what caused the mistake. They don't just recommend you; they assertively insist that their friends do business with you. They vehemently defend you when others are critical. Even if there is a good reason for the criticism, they quickly dismiss what provoked it as being an aberration or an exception.

And some take devotion even further. Some Starbucks fans refuse to drink any other coffee. Some devoted customers of Harley-Davidson tattoo the company logo on their bodies. Devoted guests of Ritz-Carlton Hotels proudly wear Ritz-Carlton-logoed clothes . . . and have the hotel chain's signature cobalt blue accessories in their homes. In these instances, magnetic service has forged a connection that becomes a part of the customer's identity and life expression.

Figuring out how to attract passionate devotion is not a simple process. There is clearly a dual "psycho-logic" factor that you must tap into. One part involves incorporating the right color, shape, sound, and touch elements into your product or service. In the customer's brain, these form an intricate pattern that links up with learned preferences, and spells attraction. The other involves providing just the right social component. Watching the Green Bay Packers alone in your living room is never the same as elbowing your way through the frozen bleachers with two hotdogs and a cold beer.

Sparking customer devotion also has to do with timing. The dimensions of the service experience that appeal to the customer today may not have the same allure tomorrow. This is more than a statement about customer fickleness. It means that customers' expectations and hopes are perpetually in motion, being reconfigured with every life experience. Likewise, customers' sense of self is always being altered, changing what excites them. It means that the rock group you would die for at twenty just doesn't hold the same appeal when you are fifty.

Another dimension that makes devotion so unpredictable has much to do with issues of context. The service experience that is seen as charming to the businessperson traveling to a hotel on holiday—a time when indulgence is rather expected—may be deemed trite or even annoying to that same businessperson staying at that same hotel for a business meeting.

Understanding the nature of magnetism from the customers' side is helpful. It tells us there is more to pulling customer devotion toward you than we service providers may be able to control. You can't turn on a tape of a cheering crowd or flood the store with the smell of motorcycle exhaust every time a customer comes into the place. Even so, there is a great deal that you can do to influence the experience the customer has with your organization. And, as with preparing for and carrying out an important first date, there are certain protocols to consider and practices to establish that are likely to yield passionately devoted customers.

The Seven Secrets of Magnetic Service

The discovery of our seven secrets of magnetic service came through intense study of a number of brands that have elicited cult-like enthusiasm. We studied companies as diverse as USAA Insurance, Universal Studios, Ritz-Carlton Hotels, the Mansion on Turtle Creek, Sewell Village Cadillac, and Harley-Davidson—all organizations that have a very large share of groupies.

We also interviewed managers, front-line employees, and some of the most devoted customers of such well-known brands as Marriott, Merrill Lynch, Sears, American Honda, Pfizer, General Electric, Holiday Inn, MBNA, Victoria's Secret, Aurora Health Care, and Washington Mutual Bank. Our intent was to look for patterns or practices that seemed to yield customer devotion. Whether the company was posh or penny pinching, the difference between remarkable and run-of-the-mill lay not with the price the customer was required to pay but rather the value the customer felt privileged to experience. We also found that though these companies used their own vocabulary to describe their approach, their values and practices were quite similar and transferable in principle to many other kinds of organizations. These shared stories led us to seven secrets for creating passionately devoted customers. We'll briefly outline them here and then develop them more fully in the rest of the book.

Secret # 1: Make Trust a Verb

The rock-bottom principle on which magnetic service is based is trust, but the basis of customer trust is always changing. Every experience the customer has with any service provider alters the standard for every other service provider. Magnetic service is malleable and agile enough to stay up on the customer's evolving requirements for trust. Trust is also multifaceted. It comes, in part, from a belief that a great service experience was not serendipitous. While customers may be infatuated by an enchanting fluke, their ongoing allegiance is anchored to the pursuit of experiences they feel can be replicated time and time again.

Trust starts with authenticity—we trust another when we perceive his or her motives are genuine or credible. Trust emanates from communication that contains crystal clear content as well as empathic "I care about you" consideration. Trust comes from a track record of promises made, paralleled with promises kept. Trust emerges as a result of demonstrated competence that leaves customers assured they are dealing with someone with the capacity to perform. Magnetic service providers work to honor and demonstrate all these features of trust in their relationships with customers.

Secret # 2: Focus on Customer Hopes, Not Just Needs

"The purpose of an organization," writes management guru Peter Drucker, "is to create and keep a customer." All the financials are just tools for keeping score of how well that purpose is being achieved. "Serving a customer" means the organization must meet customers' needs while at a minimum fulfilling their expectations of what the process will be like for getting those needs met. Perform that task adequately and you will probably survive. Perform that task well and you will probably succeed.

Magnetic service goes well beyond the "probably succeed" level. Magnetic service providers know that under the surface of the presented or obvious customer need lies the customer's hopes and wishes for what might happen. With those hopes are also aspirations, dreams, and even unconscious needs. Magnetic service providers know that tapping into this reservoir not only enables them to earn the customer's loyalty, it ensures that they solidify that loyalty by anticipating future needs. The goal here is revelation, an enriched dialogue to surface those unspoken customer aims and ambitions so that they can become the target of serving.

Secret #3: Add "Charisma" to the Service Mix

Establishing customer devotion requires taking a position that is exciting, bold, and somewhat daring. One person we interviewed told us that he felt his service was magnetic when it had an unexpected spin to it. In other words, it offered not just *more* than what the customer expected, but something *different* from what the customer expected.

There is nothing subtle about the impact of magnetic service. It hits its target in a fashion that leaves behind a positive emotional afterglow. The nature of the engagement is personal and moving. People are favorably attracted to service providers when an emotional link is created with that person. And, when that link is profound without being violating, purposeful without being manipulative, and done without presumption on your part, it makes doing business with you a treasured activity.

Secret #4: Engage the Customer's Curiosity

Customers have a huge reservoir of curiosity. Some anthropologists believe that the compulsion to learn is encoded in human DNA, which explains why humans have evolved so much further than other species. (Perhaps when God endowed humankind with a soul, the substance of that gift was curiosity!) Consequently, when service providers are alert to natural "teachable moments" in the delivery of service, they stimulate something very deep in the customer.

One way to appeal to the customer's curiosity is to create a path for participation. The allure of customer participation opportunities arises not from the fact that they *require* that customers actually join, but rather from the fact that they offer the *option* for doing so. It is the *potential* for inclusion more than the enrollment experience itself that sparks the customer's innate curiosity.

Customer participation opportunities take many forms. The most powerful actually engage the customer's energy in delivering the experience. Fresh Market grocery stores get high marks for letting customers bag, weigh, and price their own fruits and vegetables. Customers also squeeze and bottle their own orange juice and grind and package their own peanut butter. But sometimes simply enabling customers to feel and value a connection is enough to inspire their devotion.

Secret #5: Give Customers an Occasional Miracle

We have all experienced or heard about those magnetic service moments in which someone pulled out all the stops. Whether we are recipient or witness, such unexpected, out-of-the-box experiences remind us that service miracles can still happen. Such special incidents leave us as enthralled as does a table set with candles and champagne on a special date. Miracles cannot be regular fare; otherwise they become plain vanilla instead of Neapolitan. But the once-in-a-while special gesture communicates not only a desire to serve, but also a yearning to enchant.

Service miracles leave customers more emotionally moved than simply delighted; more blessed than blown away. They are at the zenith of nobility of service—special gifts that are unexpectedly bestowed and distinctively right for particular individuals. Such service miracles reflect the server's imagination; they are also manifestations of a purity of purpose. They leave customers uplifted and eager to discuss what happened with others. They are the key components of the most endearing service stories we hear and share. And with each retelling, the storyteller becomes more devoted, the audience more keen to join the fold.

Secret #6: Empower Customers Through Comfort

Customers feel empowered when they experience psychological comfort, and magnetic service provides psychological comfort by offering reliability and predictability. We can more easily deal with flights that are always late than those that are sometimes on time and sometimes not. Human nature abhors dissonance and the kind of ambiguity that makes us feel out of control. Our aversion to unpredictability means that for a service moment to be magnetic, it must be in sync with the customer's notion of what ought to happen, "congruent" as the psychologists would say—it must fit.

Customers are also empowered when service renders physical comfort—the kind that reflects a smooth operation. This means that the experience is not just hassle-free; it is noticeably comfortable, strikingly reliable, and surprisingly seamless. It requires establishing processes and systems that work with the service person in order to ensure a customer's need is met without anxiety or negative surprises. Think of it as providing service without any drag or resistance.

Secret #7: Reveal Your Character by Unveiling Your Courage

Magnetic service should reflect a deeper purpose or destiny, befitting of the organization's vision and marketplace strategy. Service with character also has a sense of innocence, naturalness, purity, and a groundedness about it. It need not be completely obvious to the customer, but it must not feel manipulative or have a quality of deviousness about it. Too often service providers, in their quest to impress customers, rely on "bait and switch" tactics, false promises, and clever tricks customers view as unfair, unnecessary, and unacceptable. The courageous service provider counts on courageous character and solid dealings to win the confidence of customers.

Magnetic service works when it emerges from the service provider's natural joy. Such service is not only clean and ethical, it is also considerate, kind, and thoughtful. It can be subtle, but if it is devoid of a childlike purity and honesty, the customer will feel they have been the subject of a ruse rather than the target of a reward.

Are You Delivering Magnetic Service?

We have outlined above some of the key concepts that characterize magnetic service. Before exploring further, it might be helpful to know where you are. Below is a list of questions to assist you in identifying your present level of service. Take a few minutes to complete the following assessment. Your honest appraisal is the first step to filling gaps in your magnetic field.

1. Do your customers believe your organization or unit listens to them more deeply than almost any organization they can think of?   Yes   No

2. Do you anticipate customers' future needs so well that customers feel you can practically read their minds?   Yes   No

3. Are customers given an opportunity to participate in a different way than they would have expected?   Yes   No

4. Does your service have sufficient consistency such that customers can trust it as being repeatable and not serendipitous?   Yes   No

5. Do customers see your organization or unit as rather daring or gallant in its approach?   Yes   No

6. Do customers think you and other employees in your organization or unit have more fun than other people?   Yes   No

7. Are customers given a chance to learn a lot simply through their encounter with your organization or unit?   Yes   No

8. Do customers witness you and others in your organization or unit perpetually improving service?   Yes   No

9. Is the interpersonal engagement with you so unforgettable that customers think positively about it again and again?   Yes   No

10. Do customers view their service experience as special, distinctive, and not the usual "beaten path" approach?   Yes   No

11. Do customers comment on how the organization or unit is almost always super comfortable to do business with?   Yes   No

12. Do customers feel completely free of dissonance and anxiety when dealing with your organization or unit?   Yes   No

13. Does your service experience reflect a deeper destiny,   Yes   No
    vision or commitment to serve?

14. Is your service to customers delivered in a way that   Yes   No
    clearly reflects a wholesome and generous attitude?

How many honest "no's" did you circle? If you circled more than three or four, you have gaps to fill, holes to repair, and practices to start. If you honestly circled all "yes's," then please give this book to someone who could use it!

Secret #1

Make Trust a Verb

magnetism \ ˈmag-nə-ˌti-zəm \ *n* : A magnet will reliably perform as it always has—its draw is one of the absolute laws of nature.

magnetic service \ mag-ˈnə-tik ˈsər-vəs \ *vb, n* : Magnetic service is trustworthy. It continually updates and reaffirms the customer's perception of reliability in the service provider.

Service is an implied agreement between the service provider and the service receiver to exchange value for value. It is also a promise by the service provider that certain core requirements will be assured and particular customer expectations will be honored. Finally, it is a pledge that should any part of the covenant not be fulfilled, the response by the service provider will represent a fair fix.

Look at the implied agreement between an airline and passenger as an example. "Mayday" Airline provides transportation to a passenger in exchange for a certain sum of money (value for value). Mayday promises that the delivery of the customer from point A to point B will be done reasonably on time, safely, and with the customer's luggage in tow. Mayday also commits that flight attendants will be helpful, snacks will be edible, seats will be tolerable, and the in-flight magazine will be complimentary. If one of these requirements or expectations is not met along the way, the airline pledges to take action to right the wrong in an appropriate fashion.

At this point you may be wondering why we chose such a seemingly obvious and elementary opening to the exploration of a concept as complex as trust. Our experience has been that many organizations falter on this vital element of magnetic service because they fail to honor the basics.

Trust Is a Moving Target

Now, for the most important part of this basic 101 intro to trust: Trust is a living thing! It is an animated, always moving dimension of all relationships, just like love. Here's why. As humans, our concept of value perpetually changes. Lots of things make value today different from value tomorrow. Apples are less valuable after you have two dozen in the cupboard than when you had none. Loud music is less valuable when you are past fifty than when you were fifteen. Making a difference becomes more valuable with maturity; making the team becomes less valuable.

If trust is a covenant of value exchange, and value is nomadic, this suggests that the pursuit of trust building needs to include some mechanism for updating the proposition. Think about expectations. Every service experience we have alters our expectations for future service. The standard for service today was altered by the service encounters we had yesterday. Customers today want every service to be FedEx fast, Amazon.com easy, Disney friendly, and Southwest Airlines thrifty. Consequently, the object of any implied covenant, agreement, promise, and pledge must be in perpetual motion. That's why we say make trust a verb—think of it as a constantly moving thing, and not a static "noun-like" concept.

Magnetic service providers know that treating trust as a moving target requires an active, ever-changing relationship with the customer. If customer expectations are part of what trust is made of, and if those expectations are in perpetual motion, then service providers must find ways to stay current. This doesn't mean that you have to be completely accurate about what customers want 100 percent of the time. It does, however, mean that your relationship with your customers must have built-in mechanisms for updating and renewal.

Trust Is Fostered by Authenticity

M.L. Leddy's is an upscale western wear store in the historic Stockyards section of Fort Worth. The store has been in the same spot since 1922 and calls itself a "handmade Texas legend." The worn wooden floor covered with antique rugs gives the appearance that many, many people have visited. The decor looks like a cross between an old West saloon and the lobby of a cowboy hotel, circa 1875. The photos that adorn the wall give you the feeling that Leddy's might have provided clothes for customers with names like Masterson, Holliday, and Earp.

Trust building starts when you cross the threshold. If you are a first-time customer, you are warmly greeted by salesman John Ripps, who confidently introduces himself, expressing sincere gratitude for your visit. If you are a repeat customer, John knows by the expression of "I'm home" on your face. His sharply focused questions enable him to very quickly zero in on your precise interests in menswear. He is warmly frank about what looks good (and not good!) on your torso and refreshingly candid in describing his experience with certain fabrics or his opinion of certain colors on you. Like a patient in an operating room, you rapidly surrender all defenses as you realize you are obviously in the hands of a pro.

John takes your measurements with the know-how of a master tailor on Fifth Avenue, New York—painstaking patience, respect, and professionalism mark his accomplished manner. Two days after any purchase, you get a handwritten personal note from John, always mentioning something you did or said. When you have something tailored or buy something that has to be specially ordered, you are likely to get an excited call: "Partner, your pants have just arrived, and they are truly gorgeous!" Repeat phone calls always yield instant recognition, warm greetings, and lots of "Yes sir, I have your measurements right in front of me," or "We'll have that shirt to you tomorrow." If he makes an error, John is boldly honest. His genuineness and sincerity make him one of the most trusted names in the business.

Trust is born out of authenticity. We trust another when we perceive his or her motives are unadulterated and credible. Think of your goal as demonstrating realness in motion. Start with an inviting, pleasant expression. Greet the customer as if you are sincerely glad to see him or her. Communicate your enthusiasm for the privilege of being of service. Look for a way to provide an early, honest, non-patronizing compliment.

Also, reveal something personal about yourself, especially something that your customer is unlikely to know. Universal Studios Hollywood puts the front-line person's favorite Universal movie on his or her nametag. It can be a great conversation starter. Many organizations include the server's hometown for the same purpose. It creates the beginning of a genuine connection and sparks an animated exchange that customers see as believable.

Trust Is Born of Demonstrated Competence

His truck looked like he'd been mud racing and lost. He slid off the seat and turned his back to the customer as he pulled up his sagging jeans and removed a shiny box of tools from behind the truck seat.

"You called for a plumber," he said with obvious pride, "And I'm your man!" With urgency he walked toward the customer with outstretched hand. The customer was already getting the happy sense that his pesky plumbing gremlins were in very deep trouble. Five minutes later, the plumber was outlining the problem, the prognosis, and the price. He spoke mostly in English, but managed to intersperse a bit of advanced plumbing lingo in his prescription. He obviously knew his stuff.

"I can fix it now . . . it'll take me an hour and a half . . . or I can come back when it's more convenient for you. You will need to take everything out of this bathroom cabinet, and I'll need to get a drop cloth and ladder from my truck."

Exactly eighty minutes later, the customer was writing a check and requesting business cards to give to friends should they ever have plumbing challenges. This customer had played "yellow pages roulette" in search of a plumber and hit the jackpot!

In order to earn the customer's trust, magnetic service providers communicate that they are worthy of trust. A person is worthy of our trust when we believe he or she has the wherewithal to actually perform what is promised or needed. Wherewithal includes competence, credential, and the correct conduct—and they all add up to credibility. We examine the plaques on the physician's wall, the badge on the police officer's uniform, or the tenor in the pilot's voice during in-flight turbulence to gain clues into matters of credibility. The plumber in the example above may have had a dirty truck but the tools of his trade were spotless.

Magnetic service providers know that credibility should be constantly kept in "demonstrator mode." Showing your competence to do the job is not about boasting; it is reminding the customer he or she made a smart decision in coming to you. It means you know how to show off without being a show off. Create your exposition of your talents from the perspective based on what your customers need; don't give them a complete catalog of what you have. Tell a personal story that uses your expertise as the backdrop, not the subject. Add to an affirmation or compliment to your customer a tidbit from your resume. For example, you might compliment your customer with, "Your jacket is gorgeous," and add, "and believe me, as a long-term collector of velvet jackets, I can spot quality."

Trust Is Enhanced Through Customer Inclusion

In a small shoe shop in a shopping mall near the New Orleans French Quarter, a cobbler sat hammering nails into the heel of a boot. He seemed completely immersed in his chore, since there were no customers to divert his concentration. The grayish sign hanging on his wall at eye level from the cash register loudly proclaimed exactly how he felt about customers. It blared out a part jesting, part serious warning:

```
┌─────────────────────────────────────┐
│  ┌───────────────────────────────┐  │
│  │                               │  │
│  │         **Price List**        │  │
│  │                               │  │
│  │      *Full soles:* $20        │  │
│  │                               │  │
│  │      *Half Soles:* $12        │  │
│  │                               │  │
│  │       *Heels:* $10            │  │
│  │                               │  │
│  │       *Taps:* $2              │  │
│  │                               │  │
│  │   Add: $3 If you wait         │  │
│  │        $5 If you watch        │  │
│  │        $10 If you try to help │  │
│  │                               │  │
│  └───────────────────────────────┘  │
└─────────────────────────────────────┘
```

Right next door to the shoe shop was a chocolate fudge shop, the kind with the big marble table in the middle and guys singing and making fudge. They were encouraging the large audience standing around to sing along as they played catch with a chocolate soft ball with one of the kids. Customers were mesmerized and enchanted as they shelled out twenty-dollar bills to purchase more fudge than they could possibly eat in a year.

Anthropologist Desmond Morris in his classic book, *The Naked Ape*, concluded that humans were genetically hardwired to be joiners, not loners. Sure there are a few hermit types who would rather live isolated than enlisted. But they are the rare exceptions. Humans have bonded in groups as long as they have walked upright. It is telling that we use solitary confinement as a punishment even within normal incarceration.

The need to connect with others is a vital part of building trust. Customers' devotion soars when they discover that they can be active participants in the service experience. At one point, we thought it was participation that accounted for zeal ("People will care if they share").

Further research has led to a profound discovery: It is the open door, not the actual participation, that fuels their trust. If the door is always open and customers know they have an opportunity to be included, the impact is almost as powerful as if they actually put "skin in the game."

Building a sense of inclusion can take many forms. Harley-Davidson created the Harley Owners Group (HOG) as a forum to bring Harley devotees together for education and recreation. Membership comes with purchase of a Harley. Frequently, members of executive management join in the fun and fellowship as HOG members reunite around a barbeque or motorcade on a Sunday afternoon. Dealers for BMW's new Mini Cooper brand automobile mail to buyers a "birth certificate" once the customer has paid a deposit. The customer is then provided with a way to follow his car's production online. Here again, customers care when they share.

Sometimes inclusion can be fun; sometimes it can have a more serious "help me" dimension. Bilijack was pursuing a company's real estate business without success. Unable to make contact with the key decision maker, he turned to his existing customers who had done business with the elusive prospect. Before long, he received a voice mail from the prospect indicating that he had been contacted by several people (Bilijack's customers) singing his praises. The next week he had a very productive first meeting with the prospect. By asking for their help, Bilijack had helped some of his existing customers feel involved in his business. Follow-up calls from them, all anxious to learn how the meeting had progressed, now telegraphed their heightened loyalty.

Inclusion reinforces a "we're in this together" partnership, and magnetic service providers are always on the lookout for novel ways to accomplish it. When Rusty Epperson at commercial real estate firm Wilson, Hull & Neal in Atlanta tours a warehouse facility with a prospect or client, for example, he often hands them the telescopic instrument used to measure the exact height of the ceiling clearance. On the business side, this measurement directly determines the client's ability to adequately rack and store additional merchandise. On the personal side, this inclusive gesture helps clients put more skin in the game, elevating their devotion and allegiance.

All these customer inclusion secrets are powerful tools for creating trust, but there are a few cautions. Provide customers a brief background when making a request for assistance so they clearly know the reason you are asking them to participate. Be clear and specific about why and how the customer can assist. "We are a bit swamped today and I could really use your assistance. If you could complete your own paperwork on this order while I get the part, I can get you processed and on your way a whole lot quicker. What do you think?"

Make certain the customer sees the opportunity to participate as a part of a larger, collective effort. The customer must see that you are sharing in the effort, otherwise he or she will feel unfairly used. Remember that the pronoun in power is "we." Give the customer plenty of breathing room. This means being selective in how and when you invite customers to participate. Too little, and the customer never gets to feel the glow of inclusion. But too much can be worse—the customer will feel intruded upon and leave thinking "they know me too well" or "they took me for granted."

Also, only ask for what is reasonable—make sure your request is something appropriate to ask of a devoted customer. Avoid any customer request that puts the organization or customer in any way at risk or in a position of liability if things go wrong. While the goal is to help the customer feel like a member of the family, it's important to remember that the customer is always the guest of the organization.

Finally, never forget to express your gratitude. Asking a customer to assist should be as unique as it is special. The customer will remember it that way if you remember to always communicate appreciation for their efforts. Customer requests should be seen as an option by the customer. Reward their caring enough to accept that option by letting them hear and feel your thanks.

Remember, too, that there are times when inclusion is inappropriate. There are times when customers do not have the skills or know-how to participate. If you go in for open heart surgery, for example, participation is not likely to be at the top of your list of hoped-for outcomes. Also, some customers do not want to be included—they want to be pampered or simply "just served." When they do, though, magnetic service providers make the path to customer contribution comfortable and obvious.

Trust Depends on Taking Risks

While it is true that trust develops with experience, it is also true that all experience begins with "no experience." Ultimately, someone without any experience with a particular relationship must take a leap of faith. So, the origin of trust is risk. When a service provider shows trust in a customer, the customer reciprocates with trust. Customer trust building requires a culture that encourages risk taking.

Arthur's is a popular deli-style restaurant in a large mall in Charlotte, North Carolina. Long known for great food and a wide range of wines, they are also known for building trust by showing trust. Customers enter the restaurant, order their food, eat, and pay as they leave. Whatever price customers tell the cashier is what is rung up on the cash register. There is no ticket, just trust.

A trust-building action can be as small as placing a cup of pennies next to the cash register with a sign that reads, "Got a penny, give a penny; need a penny, take a penny." It can be as simple as putting a sign up like the one on a dry cleaner's wall in San Diego that says, "We DO take personal checks." Examine the signs around your organization which use "Don't," "No," or other negative language. A library in Minneapolis changed "overdue fines" to "extended use fees."

What messages in your organization can be communicated in a positive, more trusting way? The magnetic power of trust is that it creates more—show trust to customers, they'll trust you back.

Trust Is Solidified Through Betrayal Management

We all know it when we experience it. Things do go wrong—the never-wear-out jeans wear out, the laundry cracks a shirt button, the steak comes to us too rare, the knock in the engine returns—and we feel let down, taken advantage of, or just plain furious. Somehow, we were counting on everything working, but the experience came up short. We have all experienced service failure—and judged the culprit by how well they responded.

Magnetic service providers know that great service recovery is not a matter of luck, or even just a matter of excellent interpersonal skills.

They treat service failure as a betrayal of trust and make sure that service recovery is planned and managed in that spirit. You may be thinking, Why not just put all your energy into doing it right the first time?' And, besides, maybe talking about mistakes will cause mistakes to happen more often. Shouldn't the goal be zero defects?

Obviously, doing preventive ("do it right the first time") maintenance on those troublesome fail points in a service delivery process is an important first step. But even the very best service operation occasionally will fail. And there are fail points in service that are just too expensive to fix. Airlines, for instance, could prevent passengers with tickets from ever getting bumped by only taking as many reservations as there are seats on the plane. But we all know that practice would make no economic sense because of the number of "no shows." So, the airlines intentionally overbook, and the consequence is that some ticketed passengers occasionally will be disappointed. Smart airlines anticipate such problems and plan effective steps to get the passengers on the next flight out. The best ones work hard to restore the customer's trust.

Customer service research has found that a customer who has had a problem elegantly corrected ends up being more loyal than a customer who has never had a problem. Before the service breakdown, the customer operated on hope. After a glitch is treated with effective betrayal management, there is proof. Proof restores trust.

Customers need to hear words and see actions that let them know you care and understand how they feel—that you appreciate why they are upset or frustrated. However, a sincere apology and empathy are not enough. Customers need to sense some urgency—words of momentum—which let them know you are working to correct their problem as quickly as possible.

It might be a good idea to think through exactly how you plan to handle breakdowns that happen with some regularity. Maybe there is merit in providing some token or gesture that tangibly telegraphs your sincere regret that the disappointment occurred. Symbolic atonement does not mean "buying" the problem. It can be as simple as offering to do a small courtesy, a personal extra, or a value-added favor. However, the most important part of trust renewal is follow-up after the problem has been resolved. This conveys to customers that you sincerely care about them and the fact that they had a problem.

Look for ways to get customer feedback about service break-downs. Keep track of the most common customer complaints. Devote time in your next meeting to talking about service recovery in terms of betrayal management. Plan ways to deal with recurring service failures as opportunities for trust renewal until they can permanently be fixed. Remember, the difference between a good service operation and a magnetic service operation is not how they perform in normal times; it's how they perform when the customer is disappointed.

· · ·

Trust is a vital building block of any relationship—be it with a friend, spouse, or customer. Trust building for the customer relationship is different, however. We generally don't "hang out" with our customers the way we do with our more intimate relations. Our friends and spouse usually know who we really are. Customers see us through the filter of commerce, contract, and compliance. The innate artificiality of the initial encounter makes trust building particularly important.

Magnetic service organizations know that suspicion can be transformed into steadfastness through the manner in which we offer to customers our authenticity, our confidence-building competence, our invitation to participate, our willingness to take a leap of faith, and our commitment to mend both association and anomaly when things go wrong.

· · ·

"Faith is not belief without proof, but trust without reservations."—Elton Trueblood

Secret #2

Focus on Customer Hopes, Not Just Needs

magnetism The characteristic force or draw of a magnetic field has a relatively short range, only impacting another object when close up.

magnetic service Magnetic service is intimate. It is grounded in an understanding of the customer's unspoken hopes, dreams, and aspirations that can only be obtained through a close, direct relationship.

There's a new computer repair service in town that customers think is awesome. It's not just that this computer repair firm really, really understands their customers' needs. They do that just fine. What makes them spectacular is their ability to look beyond customers' needs to see their unspoken hopes and unfulfilled aspirations.

PC House Call is a Dallas-based computer support firm that makes house calls. Oh, you can take your sick computer by and leave it for repair. You can even sit in their reception area and wait while they put it in their "emergency room" fast track. They will even try to help you avoid their services altogether by first attempting to troubleshoot your problem with you by phone. But what will really make you a devoted fan is PC House Call's seeming ability to read your mind!

The last time a friend of ours was in their ER reception area, owner Linda Beneventi chatted with him in between the phone calls she was fielding with her remote headset that gave her complete mobility around the shop. Quickly zipping past "How's the weather" questions, she moved on to questions that might have come from some think tank inquiry.

"Would you like to be able to interact with your laptop remotely . . . like when it's in the hotel room and you're at a meeting, would you like to be able to call it on the phone?" "How does your computer make you angry?" "Do you ever use your modem with the air phone when you're flying?" "How often do you clean your computer keys with that expensive can of air?"

If he gave Linda even the slightest "I dunno" it was parried with a friendly "Just make it up," or "What would you say if you *did* know?" Our friend suddenly realized she was asking him to dream with her.

When he got a pair of PC House Call logoed coffee cups for Christmas, the gift came with a personal note: "Thanks for what you teach us." Other service providers' cards or gifts contained the well-worn "We appreciate your business." Not PC House Call's. Linda Beneventi's stream of questions had been aimed deep beneath the immediate problem that had taken our friend to PC House Call. Now they honored him as their teacher, not just their customer.

Uncover Aspirations, Not Symptoms

Customers have needs. And underneath every need is a gap to fill or a problem to solve. Customer needs are delivered to you as warning signs or vague symptoms. Good service providers know what these symptoms are and how to fix the underlying problem. Magnetic service providers hear or see signs and symptoms and value them as real, but as only part of the story.

Magnetic service providers embrace their secret role as part

Colombo-type detective and part anthropologist. But they don't want customers to feel as though they are going through the third degree; they want customers to experience only the by-product of their intense probing. When they question customers about the symptoms and then offer a result that nails the real, deeper problem, they seem almost clairvoyant.

As Valentine's Day approached, a customer went to the greeting card section of an upscale department store to purchase a Valentine's card for his bride. The clerk warmly asked, "Would you mind telling me the mood you want your wife to be in after she reads your card?" "Amorous!" the customer replied. "What time of day were you planning to give her this card?" she continued with an impish smile. "Over dessert at the end of the evening meal I'm having delivered," he answered, rather proud of his planning.

She had one more bit of detective work to do. "Would you hope she would swoon, laugh, or blush when she reads your perfect card?" "Blush!" the customer answered, now getting excited about the evening he envisioned. "Come with me, please," she gently commanded. The clerk and the customer were soon in the lingerie section of the store. "Instead of a card, might I suggest this romantic red and white negligee with hearts in strategic places? We also have downstairs in the gourmet section a small bottle of Godiva® Chocolate Liqueur. It comes with a pair of special rose-colored cordial glasses."

The customer had gone in to spend $4 for a card (which he never got). He came out with $100 worth of gifts that would have impressed even Cupid.

The need the customer presented to the clerk was simple—he wanted a card. But the hunt was not really about a Valentine's card. That was only the symptom . . . the tip of the iceberg. He really needed to solve a problem (avoid disappointing his spouse) and fill an important desire (obtain some late-evening affection). The card might have been what he had asked for, but his real aspiration could have been met through a host of routes. The wise clerk used her questions about the perfect card to uncover his real aspirations and present a provocative alternative that left him reeling in how'd-she-know awe.

Probing for the aspirations and deeper desires beneath the customer's symptoms requires a friendly manner and a warmly curious disposition. A magnet's force operates only within a close range. The same principle applies to magnetic service providers—customers will be more open when they feel a close connection to you. Notice the style of the clerk. She built rapport through warm and obvious interest in the customer's quest. She was careful not to invade the customer's privacy, but was noticeably eager to learn the customer's real intentions.

The customer's original request must remain the centerpiece of the discussion; otherwise the customer will not believe you think it is serious. If the clerk had said, "Are you SURE you want a Valentine's card?" the customer might have responded with a snide, "Did I mumble?" If the clerk had diverted him too soon to lingerie or gourmet spirits, her actions would have seemed like manipulative up selling. Instead, she provided an enchanting adventure.

Try to make your line of questioning a charming, even fun, trip for the customer. The department store clerk kept her customer guessing about what she would ask next. While your quest is to make a deeper discovery, it must sound to your customer like a simple exploration or confirmation of what he or she has in mind.

Tie Customer History to the Future

A guest of the Ritz-Carlton Hotel in Naples, Florida, was attending a two-day conference. Since his two children had a school holiday and his wife was working, he brought his children with him on the trip. After a nice dinner in the hotel restaurant, the waiter asked if they would like anything else. "Popcorn!" squealed his two kids. They had planned an after-dinner pay-per-view movie for the three of them! "Certainly," said the waiter and minutes later brought in a large container of freshly popped popcorn. A year later, the man was in the same hotel for a meeting without his children. As he was asking for the check, the mâitre d' approached him and asked if he'd like some popcorn again!

Sometimes the service encounter is fortunate enough to be backed up by history—previous moments with the customer. Smart organizations make a record of those moments to create opportunities to personalize later experiences. Customer record keeping need not be as sophisticated as Ritz-Carlton Hotel's famous guest preference system.

An old fashioned "note card" system can be just as effective. Make notations of incidents that your customer would be pleased you remembered, not shocked that you knew. You don't want your attempt to personalize service to be perceived as an invasion of privacy—a major "big brother is watching" experience that will cause the customer to leave "because they knew me too well."

An effective way to balance the personalized service/privacy invasion issue is to let the customer know how you knew. When a couple sat down at their favorite restaurant, the waiter brought a special bottle of wine. "I remembered the last time you were here you mentioned that you would be coming back for your birthday. We wanted to do our part to make it special." This helps make the occasion memorable without the customer spending the evening preoccupied with "how'd they know . . . and what else do they know?"

Rely on Values, Not Features

The concept of "serving a customer," by definition, carries a connotation of making a contribution and offering a gift. We "offer" service; we don't provide service as though it were some physical object simply to be handed over. Magnetic service providers search for a nobler platform from which to launch their contribution.

When the service experience touches a key personal value of the customer, he or she is not only motivated to come back for more, he or she is "called" to devotion. Granted, there are service offerings that aren't easily "noble-ized." What's the deep emotional value in getting your car washed or your dry cleaning done? Most customer aspirations, though, spring from deep values that are often obvious even to a bystander. When people boycotted Exxon over the Valdez oil spill, Ford over the failure of Explorers or Jack-in-the-Box over the outbreak of *E.coli*, there was more in the mix than a concern for health or dissatisfaction over lapses in quality. On the positive end of the value spectrum, some people buy Ben and Jerry's ice cream because of the company's stand on protecting the environment, or swear by Body Shop cosmetics because of the company's role in promoting trade in underdeveloped countries.

Use Collective Customer Dreaming

Customer focus groups have been around for many years, and were originally used as a tool of the consumer products world. Marketing departments asked a group of customers about their reactions to everything from "How does it taste?" to "How much would you pay for it?" Only recently have marketers begun to use customers to dream of unintended applications. Customers enjoy collective dreaming or "dreaming with you" if given an opportunity.

Collective customer dreaming starts with capitalizing on a setting and occasion in which the customer is in the mental space to dream. There are often "moments of sleep" when collective customer dreaming can appropriately occur. "Moments of sleep" is a figurative way to describe those customer contact times when there is a natural wait involved. One inventive self-service car wash manager asked customers if he could sit in the car with them and ask them a few questions as they waited for their car to wash. A restaurant manager interviewed customers after they had placed their dinner order. These are natural "moments of sleep." Never talk about "dreams" when the customer is "wide awake"—that is, actively engaged in the act of getting service.

And there are times the customer may be available for dreaming but not in the mood for dreaming. The intensive-care waiting room might be a nice quiet setting for talking about hopes and aspirations, but it is not likely to be a good context for the topic. Likewise, if the period of customer inactivity is viewed as a negative, introducing a "while you are waiting" inquiry might yield more disdain than delight. No one likes to be reminded of a service delay they thought was inappropriate to start with.

How do you initiate collective customer dreaming? Start with a dreamlike setup with the customer—for example, indicate that you are building a fantasy, doing some really, really long range planning, or writing a futuristic article on your industry. "We have been having fun over lunch trying to imagine what branch banking might be like in ten years. We've heard some pretty wild stuff. We decided to let some of our best customers join in the fun. We think this will help us plan for the future needs of our customers. If you are up for a minute of fun and wildness while you are waiting, I'd like to ask you're a couple of questions."

Then, ask questions that help your customers get into the act of "futuring" with you. Always craft questions in the "what might be" not in "what would be." Real dreams always blend the real and precise with the odd and peculiar; what is with what might be. The intent is not to create definites and absolutes, but tentative, partially baked ideas. No matter what the customer's answer, provide affirmation and support. The most inane answer just might have brilliance behind it if developed a bit. Select questions like the ones below:

- What is something no one in our industry is doing that you would like to see someone do?

- If you were redesigning the way this service was delivered and you only cared about (pick an attribute . . . saving money, speed, hassle-free service, etc.) how might you do it differently?

- If we hired a bunch of kids to advise us on how to make our service better, what might they tell us?

- Who gives you the best service you have ever gotten anywhere? What if we wanted to be *the* (their exemplar) of (your industry)? What might that look like?

- If our service were a sport, what sport would it be? What might you prefer it to be?

Depend on Dialogues, Not Interviews

Every sixty days, twelve eBay users are invited to journey to San Jose, California, to participate in the company's "Voice of the Customer" program. These select people visit almost every department to talk about ways to improve service. This focus group methodology goes one step further. Every month thereafter, for six months, these same users are reassembled to explore emerging issues. As these eBay customers evolve from feeling like mere interviewees to members of the company, they get bolder in their input and more strident in their allegiance. The by-product of these customer-devotion creating conversations has been important service enhancements for eBay.

Duke Energy has used a "Boards of Customers" program in the

regions they serve. These "experienced" customers volunteered their time each quarter to act as sounding boards for new products and services. They also became a key neighborhood conduit for feedback and ideas on improvement. Not only did the chosen member's experiences lead to greater devotion to the company, it also provided them with unique opportunities to become advocates for the Charlotte, North Carolina-based utility.

Learn From What You See, Not Just What You Hear

"We will give you a 25 percent discount on your room rate," the front desk hotel clerk pleasantly said to the frequent guest, "if you'll let us watch you unpack!" When the guest recoiled in disbelief, the perky clerk quickly added with a mischievous smile, "No, it's not what you think! We're not trying to get kinky; we're just trying to learn how our guests actually use our guest rooms. As soon as you're unpacked we promise to leave you in privacy!"

Ten customers later, the hotel had learned a lot about subtle workarounds—those awkward hotel-room distractions customers cope with, yet never complain about. Having the complimentary hair dryer already plugged into the bathroom receptacle meant that guests who wanted to use their own dryer had to go through the hassle of unplugging it. The couple traveling together had to put one suitcase on the floor because only one luggage cradle was provided. The iron cleverly attached to the ironing board left no square ironing board corner for pressing the shoulders of dress shirts. And having phones placed only by the bedside made plugging the phone line into a laptop computer to check e-mail extremely awkward for traveling business people. None of these subtle but off-putting workarounds had ever appeared on guest comment cards.

A similar dynamic was found in the health care industry. When University of Florida Professor Gerald Young asked patients the reasons why they would switch physicians or health care providers, "quality of care" was first; "personal treatment" was third. But when Dr. Young asked the same patients who then actually switched physicians or health care providers about their reasons for doing so, "personal treatment" moved up to first place; "quality of care" fell much lower. Customers' predictions of their behavior were quite different from how they actually performed.

So, should you stop asking for feedback and throw out interview data as irrelevant? Absolutely not. Consider predictive data as an incomplete early warning system. Then, add observation to your list of customer learning methods. As Yogi Berra said, "Sometimes you can't see for looking." Smart service providers are disciplined in their observations.

Listening for hopes and aspirations is truly a contact sport, not a research project. Market research and survey results give you data, not loyalty; information, but not devotion. The late Stanley Marcus, cofounder of Neiman Marcus, once said, "A market never purchased a single item in one of my stores, but a lot of customers came in and made me a rich man!"

. . .

Customer devotion is built on face-to-face engagement laced with straight talk and obvious responsiveness. Discovering hopes, not just stated needs, happens when, as David Welch of Prologis Trust in Atlanta characterizes it, "you are curious enough to get behind the questions the customer is really asking."

Eighty-five percent of customers who leave an organization, when asked, say they were satisfied with the organization they abandoned. "Customer satisfaction" buys you little in today's competitive economy. If you want a devoted customer—one who champions you to others, forgives you for mistakes, and stays loyal despite price increases—then get in close and look beneath the customer's stated needs and obvious expectations. Your seemingly clairvoyant understanding of their hopes, aspirations, and unstated desires will draw them even closer to you and allow you to develop an ever-expanding repertoire and reputation for magnetic service.

. . .

"A guest sees more in an hour than the host in a year."
—Polish proverb

Secret #3

Add "Charisma" to the Service Mix

magnetism A magnetic force only interacts with physical materials that can conduct electricity.

magnetic service Magnetic service is electrifying. It interacts with customers in a way that conveys excitement, releases passion, and invites customer energy into the relationship.

Customers like dealing with employees who are committed; they adore dealing with employees who are not just passionate, but also give their service charisma. The word "charisma" originates from the Greek word "charizesthai" which means "to favor." The theological connotation is "a divinely conferred gift or power."

Charisma is a form of personal magnetism, a special kind of appeal or charm. Charismatic service is the creation of a customer experience that is so uniquely charming that customers are captivated (the root word being "to capture"). It is service that "sparkles." It is loaded with a kind of infectious energy—an energy that invites reciprocal energy from the customer. It is the Francie Johnsen approach to magnetic service.

Francie Johnsen is an Eckerd's pharmacist in Dallas who customers label "the fastest pharmacist in the West." Watching Francie in action is like watching ducks swimming on a pond—under the water you see frenzied feet; on top you only see grace. To customers, Francie never appears rushed despite the breakneck speed of her hands as she sets the pharmacology record for minimum time taken to fill prescriptions.

Francie manages customers' wait in a way that leaves them infatuated. "Chip," she said one day, "go and check to see if your pictures are ready while I fill your script." "But, Francie," Chip protested, "I don't have pictures being developed." Unchanged by his refusal to take the bait, she elevated the tease to a higher altitude. "Well, go look at someone else's pictures . . . or better yet, go check your blood pressure on that machine over there. I'll have your order ready by the time you get back."

The whole store began to sparkle when Francie came to town. Other departments started to reflect her super-positive, always teasing, and playful style. Even the sometimes gruff kid at the photo lab demonstrated a propensity for communicating joy. Before Francie came on board, should you have had a prescription called in or dropped off for later retrieval, you would have received a mechanical "someone in this household has a prescription ready for pickup" message on the answering machine. She put a stop to that. Afterward, when the vet called in a prescription to Eckerd's for Chip's cat, the answering machine at Chip's house played an even more personalized message: "Taco, meow, meow," the message pronounced with Francie's voice said, "Tell your parents, meow, meow, that your prescription is ready, meow, meow!" Not only did she call the cat, she spoke fluent kitty!

Service with Charisma Is Passionate

"Charisma" should be Fred Givhan's middle name. Owner, president, and chief morale officer of Direct Connect, Fred is Mr. Spirited. Some might say he's "sometimes wrong but never in doubt"; some might say he needs to cut way back on his daily coffee intake. But no one would ever say Fred is not passionate about Direct Connect. All his employees—mostly technical folks—personify the exact same attitude, although not as noisily. Even his dog, who his wife and office manager, Martha, occasionally brings to work, reflects the same "I'm so excited" style.

Walk into the Direct Connect premises and the thing you'll hear first is Fred in the front corner (right at the storefront window) talking on the phone or to a live customer with animation and interest. The second thing you'll notice is the big sign on the wall that reads:

Direct Connect Motto

On each and every appointment it is within our power with the ingredients on hand to make the world's most delectable chicken salad or the most putrid batch of chicken sh*t!

At $95 per hour it is our obligation to accomplish our task of serving the customer a delectable experience or we do not deserve to be paid. The customer is not expected to be any more a part of the process than they wish!

What is your experience with Direct Connect? First, you get absolute barebones honesty about what might be wrong with your computer—no diplomacy involved. You are allowed to go back with the technicians and watch them take a peek inside if you like—they even let you help! The most common phrase you hear from a tech is: "We'll drop it by your house or office." Work is done at lightning speed, always with the quality obsession of the little old watchmaker. And every person in the organization loves to teach customers what he or she knows. The most common customer expression as they leave the shop: ". . . And I thought I was enthusiastic!"

Secret #3: Add "Charisma" to the Service Mix

"There is an energy field between humans," wrote philosopher Rollo May, "and when you reach out in passion it is met with an answering passion and changes the relationship forever." This is one of our favorite quotes and it tells a powerful story: Passion is contagious. Passion is fundamentally a gift that connects with the generosity tendency in another. When we are on the receiving end of passion, we feel favored by the "extra helping" nature of the connection, as though the passionate person is giving us more than normal.

Passion is not necessarily noisy. Passionate people often display enthusiasm and energy, but some are quiet about it. Passion is about fervor and zeal. It lies at the opposite end of the spectrum from apathy. Passion is determination and focus. Passion is a "making something happen" type of investment. It may well up in us as emotion and feeling but it spills out of us as resolve and old-fashioned grit. Michelangelo, Thomas Edison, and Mother Teresa were all passionate and none of them showed an overexcited disposition.

What does charismatic service look like from the passionate side of the picture? An eighty-year-old patient was extremely anxious since her two dogs were home alone while she was in Aurora Health Care's Memorial Hospital of Burlington, Wisconsin. While she had arranged for a neighbor to walk the dogs and feed them each day, she still worried about their welfare. The patient's nurse, concerned about the patient's anxiety and passionate about giving magnetic service, contacted the neighbors and arranged to go to the patient's home and take photos of the patient's two dogs so she could see they were doing fine. The patient's anxiety evaporated.

Passion comes from an inner space of generosity. Oden's Dock in Cape Hatteras, North Carolina, is famous for their abundance mentality. Their being a dock/restaurant/hotel combination enables them to fashion special service across several types of customers. Oden's Dock customers get a free beer token for use in Oden's Breakwater restaurant bar. Hatteras Harbor Motel customers who use the dock get free coffee with their wake-up call, the service of a dock boy to transport luggage to their boat, and a free newspaper and fishing advice (on request), delivered either to their hotel room or boat. There's always a person on the dock to catch dock lines when a boat backs into a slip. "A small favor almost always pays off big," says co-owner and operator

Dan Oden. "Plus, we just take great pride in giving our customers a unique brand of service. That's why they return, year after year, and we are always happy to see them."

Service with Charisma Is Inventive

People who deliver charismatic service are so propelled by a commitment to goal achievement that they are undeterred by normal barriers. Barriers are viewed not as sources of disappointment or as obstacles to be eliminated but as opportunities for creativity. Inventiveness entails trading in the tried and true for the novel and new.

The old story of the slow elevators demonstrates this perspective. A new high-rise office building had tenants complaining that the elevators were too slow. One consulting engineer pursued the obvious and suggested to the building owners that they speed up the current elevators or add a new one. Another engineer suggested they stagger starting, ending, and lunch times so tenants wouldn't all be using the elevators at the same time. An inventive engineer suggested they put mirrors in the lobbies on all the floors. His solution was implemented. People were thereafter so enthralled with looking at themselves and others in the mirrors that they did not notice the wait.

Pure inventiveness is fueled more by a playful attitude than a courageous one. It is an act of resourcefulness. Re-source-ful literally means "full of the capacity to re-source, or get back to the creative origins of something." This entails seeing things through the lens of innocent curiosity. Einstein is credited with saying, "Genius is born of the innocent ingenuity of a child."

Magnetic service providers nurture a "never say die" attitude. But they also embody a spirit that says, "We'll outsmart our competition." Take resolve and resourcefulness and you have the particular inventiveness you get from magnetic service providers who like to spice up their service recipe with a large helping of charisma.

BAGCO is an industrial and medical plastic bag manufacturer and distributor. One of their customers, baby products distributor Lansinoh, approached owner Nossi Taheri with a challenge. Lansinoh was in the market for a bag that could be attached to a breast pump to catch and then store a mother's milk. Other bag distributors had attempted to sell Lansinoh on the bags they had. Nossi probed more deeply to learn the customer's aspirations of how the bag would be used. First, he learned the obvious: They were looking for a bag that could be sealed and later dropped into a baby's nursing bottle. But Nossi sensed there was much more that others had missed.

"We need a bag that can be stood on its end even if it is partially full—mothers don't always produce exactly six ounces. It might only be an ounce," said the customer. Nossi continued to probe. He learned that many of the nutrients a new baby needs from its mother's milk are left in the form of a film that sticks inside the bag. "It may not be possible," dreamed the customer, "but we'd really like the bag to empty every drop of nutrients when in use."

Nossi was driven by a desire to delight the customer. Fortunately, he was an inventive person, holding several patents for innovative bag designs. He formulated a completely different type of plastic and invented a bag that would exactly meet the customer's hopes. The president of Lansinoh was completely blown away. The footnote to the story is that Lansinoh now distributes Mother's Milk® all over the world and BAGCO has all of their bag business.

Service with Charisma Is Touching

Touch is a very big word. It covers so many dimensions. It can mean physical contact ("She touched him on his arm."). It might mean emotional impact ("That movie touched me."). It can mean a hint ("Add a touch of mint."). It can also mean a link ("Let's stay in touch."). Roll all these meanings together and you have the essence of a bond or connection. Charismatic service touches you in a fashion that bolsters a bond. It can be as subtle as a friendly wink or as big as a bear hug. The key is you feel it, like it, and remember it.

A large public library in the middle of a large northeastern city wanted to add a little extra to the service experience of their patrons— a touch! The checkout clerk was instructed to look patrons directly in the eye and make some physical contact as books were being checked in or out—a handshake, a pat on the arm, or a gentle tap on the wrist.

But only on Mondays, Wednesdays, and Fridays. On Tuesdays, Thursdays, and Saturdays, there was to be only eye contact. Outside the front door, a researcher was waiting to ask exiting patrons to rate the library on a one-to-ten scale. The Monday-Wednesday-Friday patrons gave the library considerably higher marks than the Tuesday-Thursday-Saturday patrons.

Now, before you rush to some bizarre conclusion that has front-line people attending "customer hugging" classes, know that the issue is not about invading the personal space of unsuspecting strangers. It is about making connections. People are favorably attracted to service providers when there is an emotional link with them. Emotional connections that are properly established amplify affection.

Chip and his wife, Nancy, were guests at the legendary Hotel Del Coronado in San Diego. It was a special getaway, having involved lots of planning. They checked in during the middle of the afternoon, and the bellman escorted them up to their room. Unfortunately, it was far from the special room they had expected. Sensing the Bells' displeasure, the bellman said, "You are not pleased with your accommodations, are you?" Chip explained that they had prepaid for an ocean *front* room with a king-size bed, not an ocean *view* room with two double beds. "Let me see what I can do," he said. "I'll be right back."

Minutes later he returned and stated that the front desk clerk had made a mistake. However, the proper room was not yet cleaned. He invited Chip and Nancy to either remain in the room for an hour or so, when he would return to move them, or to take a nice walk on the beach, during which he would move their luggage for them, leaving their new room key at the front desk. They were beginning to feel better about their situation.

That evening, they had an elegant dinner in the hotel restaurant. They had been back in their room for only a few moments when there was a knock on the door. It was the same bellman. "I thought you might enjoy a nightcap . . . " he said as he looked Chip in the eye and warmly extended his hand, " . . . with our apologies." He had asked the restaurant what before-dinner drinks the Bells had ordered and had them duplicated as their before-bed treat! Now when they think of the Hotel Del, the bellman's special gesture is even more vividly remembered than the distinctive beauty of the hundred-year-old landmark hotel.

What made this incident such a touching experience? The bellman sensed Chip and Nancy's displeasure on entering the wrong room—his antenna was up very high as he stayed connected to their non-verbal signals. He confronted the front desk clerk out of their earshot. Had he used the bedside phone for his "we have a problem" discussion, it might have further intensified the disharmony.

He was boldly truthful about what had happened. He gave no excuses, no "this was an exception" explanation, no lengthy justifications. He provided options—and stayed in control of the resolution. The Bells' anxiety was lowered by knowing that he was not delegating the solution to someone else, but rather that he was staying on the case himself. After all, why bring in another relationship when he was well on his way to creating a powerful bonding experience?

The bellman looked for a personalized solution, one that was congruent with the "romantic" purpose of their stay. Bringing Chip and Nancy a coupon for a complimentary future stay, or instructing the housekeeper to leave extra mints at turndown service, would not have had the same feel as bringing the Bells their special preference in beverages. He was assertive in his apology and authentic in his handshake. The bottom line: What made his gesture magnetic was his special touch—a heart-to-heart connection that communicated "I care about you, I care about this hotel, and I care about your memory of this experience."

Establishing connections with customers is about creating a link, not just about making contact. It is about stirring customers' emotions, not just getting their attention. This means the process must be laced with spirit, energy, and attitude. But creating a bond works only when the customer voluntarily responds or is involuntarily moved. This suggests that they are experiencing the connection as out of the ordinary without being out of harmony. If the customer is expecting a smile and gets a smile plus a handshake, you win. But, if the unsuspecting customer also gets a big bear hug, you will probably not win. Figuring out the right balance takes being alert to a customer's verbal and nonverbal cues.

We live in a time of cultural diversity. Differing norms and mores mean that bonding activities must be tailored to each individual. Gender, race, and age influence what is appropriate in any given instance. Hugging your mother might be OK nearly all of the time. But hugging your drill sergeant in boot camp, or the IRS agent during your tax audit, might evoke less than an enthusiastic response. These are all things to keep in mind when trying to reach out and touch your customer.

What else makes bonding charismatic? It is charismatic when it makes you, as well as your customer, smile. It is charismatic when it makes you, as the service provider, look forward to its execution with the excitement of a nine-year-old waiting for Santa. It is charismatic when the customer wants to tell others about the experience. It is charismatic when it stays in customers' memory banks for some time afterward . . . or, if it quickly surfaces in your customer's mind when your name or the name of your organization is mentioned.

A Dallas restaurant that is famous for its lively ambiance and surprising frivolity often has waiters applaud when a repeat customer enters the restaurant. That might be an embarrassing gesture at a four-star fancy place, but it fits well with the wildness of Celebration West. A major hospital in the Midwest asks patients what their favorite flower is. When a patient returns to the hospital, staff arrange for a single stem of that flower to be placed on the patient's bed stand. The forty-cents-a-stem cost pales in comparison to the devotion that arises in the patient as a result of the acknowledgment. The Four Seasons Hotel in Austin is a pet-friendly hotel. Should guests announce they are bringing their cat, for instance, they are enchanted when they check into their room and find a Four Seasons-logoed pet food and water bowl on a place mat, with a complimentary cat toy.

Bonding must fit the situation. The customer bond must make sense in its context. Offering a complimentary bottle of champagne at a fast food restaurant would be as dissonant as handing out a free serving of french fries at a five-star restaurant. But creating a congruent connection is about more than making sure the conditions are appropriate. It is about carrying things out with the proper tone and style. As a former service quality instructor at the Disney Institute put it: "Disney makes magic with pixie dust. Whatever they do smells right, tastes right, sounds right, and feels right." Bonding creates passionately devoted customers when all of the elements fit together.

· · ·

Even really great service can fail to have magnetic attraction if it is bland or spiritless. Magnetic service works when it has the type of charisma that compels the customer to join and return. It achieves this when the experience is passionately delivered, cleverly inventive, and resonates with the customer at a deep emotional level.

E. M. Forster wrote in his classic book, *Howard's End*, "Only connect." This was an invitation to rely on the power of passion, the gift of creativity, and the joy of mutuality. Customers move from the transience of "I shall return" to the permanence of "I do" when their union with a service provider touches their essence and not just their assets.

· · ·

"You want pistols, hot-blooded people bent on making their mark. Not mild-mannered, conforming types who will succumb to the awesome power of the existing culture."—Price Pritchett

Secret #4

Engage the Customer's Curiosity

magnetism A type of natural magnet is a rock called magnetite, which was also called lodestone, or "leading stone."

magnetic service Magnetic service gently leads the customer into service encounters that result in customer learning.

Tulemar Bungalows is a enchanting getaway. Nestled on the side of a mountain in a rainforest that overlooks the Pacific Ocean near Quepos, Costa Rica, it features an array of upscale octagon-shaped tree houses, an infinity-edge swimming pool for breathtaking ocean sunsets, and a first-class open air restaurant.

We were there with our wives for the Christmas holidays. After a lengthy afternoon jungle ride, we returned for a Christmas dinner fit for a king. The meal featured an assortment of unique, local dishes all elegantly prepared and exquisitely presented. However, our favorite dish was a John Dory fish, pan-fried in a ravishing and unique combination of tropical fruits and spices.

"The fish was excellent," one of us commented to our waiter as he brought the next course of delicacies. "What's in that dish?"

"I think with some mango and mustard," he responded in broken English. We contemplated how we could learn more detail about this special delicacy. Minutes later our dreams were fulfilled.

The head chef appeared at our table with a copy of the cherished recipe. But our lesson did not stop there. He spent five minutes offering a few cautions, shortcuts, and embellishments. He even asked a waiter to bring over the bottle of the wine he used so we could see the label. As he warmly bid us farewell to return to his kitchen we looked at each other in quiet amazement. Finally, one of us broke the silence: "We've all been to chef's school!"

While "tutor me or lose me" is not yet the byword of today's customer, their expectation that service providers be super smart has fast become a standard. Call center employees get dinged by customers much more quickly for inadequate knowledge than for rudeness. In fact, most people nowadays would rather have a surly expert than a polite idiot. What's more, we want to become virtual experts ourselves. We want software that not only instructs us in application but offers us insights into new possibilities. In addition to assembly instructions, we also want to know about maintenance, add-on features, and access to information on upgrades.

Quenching customers' thirst for knowledge is an interesting enough challenge for organizations with products that already provide built-in opportunities. Doing so is even more challenging for service businesses. But service providers like Tulemar Bungalows' head chef know how to create edifying educational experiences. There are many ways they do so, but they all start by understanding and respecting the customer's innate desire to learn.

Honor the Customer's Natural Curiosity

Customers enter all service encounters with curiosity. Unheard by the service provider, the customer's self-talk nosily asks non-stop questions:

"Will I get my needs met?" "How will I be treated?" "Will this be different from last time?" or "Why do they do it like that?" Magnetic service providers know that customer curiosity is a powerful force that can be converted into customer learning. And the customers who derive learning from service providers pay the tuition with their devotion.

Customer curiosity must first be honored in order for it to be unveiled and mobilized. Instead of having a "we know what's best" attitude, wise service providers respond to the curt or confused customer inquiry with, "What a great question!" Astute physicians who recognize when a patient is puzzled know that there is a noisy internal monologue behind those eyes of uncertainty. Shelving any hint of condescension or indifference, they shift into a slower pace, acting more as guide than guru, more as partner than parent. Mixing medicine with mentoring, they help patients become knowledgeable and gain patient loyalty in the process.

Honoring the customer's curiosity means making your respect for that curiosity obvious. It entails capitalizing on each opportunity in which customers might have something to learn. Like teachers who know to "start where the student is," service providers who honor customer curiosity also treat each customer encounter as a unique experience and exhibit body language that speaks of acceptance and affirmation. They suspend any superior or judgmental attitudes that might put the customer's growth in jeopardy. They are receptive, impeccably honest, and exhibit obvious congruence between word and deed.

Ask Thought-Provoking Questions

At MidAmerican Energy's Customer Care center in Davenport, Iowa, telephone reps are trained to listen for opportunities to teach customers more about energy conservation. "What else can I help you with?" can lead to more service; "What else can I help you learn?" can lead to deeper loyalty.

Brainstorm questions you believe will engage your customer's curiosity. Consider queries about your customer's *customer* as one particularly promising avenue for insight. Asking your customer a question like "What keeps *your* customer up at night?" may initially evoke a blank stare. But it can start your customer's mental wheels turning.

When you conduct focus groups or interviews with customers, always ask participants to dream with you—Ask "What are ways we can make your life better in a fashion that no one like us is presently doing?"

Use Insight-Producing Protocols

A team of financial advisors in the Private Client Division of the Charlotte, North Carolina, office of Merrill Lynch decided to add a form of educational engagement to their offerings. Taking the first letter of the last name of three financial advisors in the team, they set up the CBC Group. The CBC Group prides itself in delivering great customer service. They also view their role as financial mentors, building customer loyalty by building customer competence. "We have found that the best customer is an educated customer," says Tom Berger, the "B" in the CBC handle. "Most of our customers are good at doing what they do to earn the money we help them manage. Most are not experts on investment strategies. We view our job as helping them get smarter about financial management. That way, we can partner with them in making wise decisions. We see every contact as an opportunity to leave our customers smarter than before."

The CBC Group has instituted a set of protocols to ensure that customer learning is hardwired into every encounter. Most conversations end with a thought-provoking question. Correspondence includes information that helps teach, not just inform. Financial plans contain a primer on elements of sound long-range financial planning. E-mails are thoughtful and instructive; online access to customer account information leaves the user more confident as well as more competent. The entire customer relationship is managed with the intent of keeping the customer's curiosity fully engaged.

Create Smart Processes

Seafood fans love Jim White's Half Shell in Atlanta. Owner-operator Clay Perritt treats his staff exactly the way he wants his staff to treat customers, constantly on the lookout for ways to learn more about them and have them get to know him better. Example? Perritt created a simple but smart process to ensure that repeat customers keep returning. Customers who come back are treated as though they are part of a family returning to the restaurant to eat together. They are not only given the best servers, almost without fail but they are given the same servers each time. Like mothers at Thanksgiving dinner, servers know the nuances of everyone's preferences, right down to a particular taste in food or a favorite drink. The consistent familiarity between server and customer and server and operator creates opportunities for everyone to get to know each other better. The smart processes here breed a special "welcome back home—you and your family belong here" type of magnetism.

Consider the experience of most first-time guests at the elegant Grove Park Inn Resort and Spa in Asheville, North Carolina, nestled at the foothills of the Blue Ridge Mountains. It would appear that everywhere a guest goes—from indoor pool to restaurant to golf course—every hotel employee seems to be able to call that guest by name. That is not accidental. The Grove Park Inn Resort and Spa prides itself in creating a setting akin to an idyllic country club where guests are almost like members. Employees subtly, and out of the sight of the guests, remind each other of guests' names. The company holds strongly to values such as the importance of providing legendary service, being ethical, working hard, adopting a "consider it done" attitude, and being consistent. The way they manage these elements turns them into what amounts to proprietary techniques—service attributes that are unique to them. Adhering to such values inspires employees to do the little things, like remembering a name. The bottom line is that guests experience Grove Park as a classy ninety-year-old inn with old-world charm, exceptional service, and a welcoming, comfortable atmosphere.

A key concept in magnetic service is to leave the customer impressed with what you know. While invading privacy is obviously a no-no, when it comes to knowing about your customers, familiarity does not breed contempt. It breeds devotion.

Promote Hard-Wired Wisdom

We are on the verge of the "smart everything" era. Our automobiles tell us when to change the oil; our online grocery store suggests we check our stock of condiments ("You should be almost out of salt"), and our desktop computers cue us when our mother-in-law's birthday is approaching. Hotels remember our preferences in pillows, pizza deliverers remember our favorite toppings, and express mail carriers know right where we leave the package for pickup. Before too long, our microwave will be asking our refrigerator, "What's for dinner?" and our air conditioner will tell our tub, "Start a hot bath!" when they detect our vehicle approaching home.

As customers come to anticipate having learning components "built in" to products, they will extend that expectation to include all facets of the customer encounter. Wise organizations will ensure that "smartness" is subtly woven into the very fabric of their offerings. *Turned On* coauthor, speaker, and Marriott International General Sales Manager Roger Dow puts it this way: "It's not enough that we impress our customers, we must instruct them as well. And since we usually can't teach them directly, we must embed learning in how we serve them." This means thinking about the customer encounter from the inside out, not just the outside in. A magazine ad for myCIO.com (now McAfee ASaP) depicts a baseball on the living room floor with a cracked window in the background, obviously the aftermath of some neighborhood Little Leaguer's home run. The caption reads, "What if the baseball could repair the window?" This reflects the "inside out" thinking needed to embed learning into the service experience.

Examine every aspect of your customer's service encounter with your unit. Ask the Roger Dow question: How can we engage the customer's curiosity and embed a learning outcome into this service experience? A training company turned their course evaluation form into a tool to review key learning points in the course. Handouts offered a sidebar on how to get the most out of a small group discussion. They even put fun facts related to the course on the Styrofoam® coffee cups in the training center break area. Their goal was to examine everything the customer touches, uses or sees through the lens of "How can I make my customers smarter?"

Share Unique DNA Competencies

"Don't just share what you are good at," preached a CEO to his sales reps at their preconvention meeting. "Share the *essence* of what you are good at." The words were a familiar refrain to the audience. An outsider would have been puzzled by the challenge.

An explanation as to what the CEO meant has to do with the fact that certain competencies lie behind the skills the customer sees. Think of the CEO's challenge in this way: What would you be good at if you left your organization and your industry for a completely different industry? Suppose you left your organization to work in the Peace Corps. What would be your answer if the recruiter asked you, "What is it, work-wise, that you are good at that we might be able to use?"

Great front desk clerks obviously are good at checking people into a hotel. But their DNA competencies include things like a flair for offering warm hospitality, the capacity to multi-task, and the ability to exhibit grace under pressure. Nurses have all manner of medical knowledge. But among their DNA competencies is the ability to cope with extremely diverse interpersonal encounters. In the same five minutes, a nurse might assist a depressed patient who just learned his condition is terminal, a new mother who just heard that she had a baby girl, and a young child experiencing major pain.

The question is this: Are there ways to share DNA competencies in a fashion that uniquely benefits customers?

A real estate company held a show-and-tell team-building activity at their annual company picnic. People were asked to share with others the part of their job they most enjoyed. They then formed groups with others who enjoyed the same things to create an imaginary company that maximized the use of their "most enjoyables." So many people identified "complex problem solving" as their most enjoyable work that the company decided it was a pervasive enough DNA competency that they would create a new hotline trouble-shooting unit. Agents around the country could channel tough client questions to one of the company's designated complex-problem solvers for smart resolution. A "Stump the Broker" feature was soon added to the company's Web site for online access to these master problem solvers. The "smart people serving smart people" unit was so successful that it was soon copied by other real estate companies.

CHEP Equipment Pooling Systems, headquartered in Orlando, Florida, is one of the largest leasers of pallets, platforms on which goods are stored, in the food industry. Instead of owning and maintaining pallets, a food producer or distributor leases them from CHEP for a fraction of the purchase and maintenance cost. Obviously, to move millions of pallets around the country requires extraordinary competence in logistics, and CHEP shares that competence in out-of-the-ordinary ways. When a CHEP sales team called on a very large retailer in northwest Arkansas, they brought along one of their resident logistics gurus. Instead of giving a sales pitch focusing on "what CHEP can do for you," the team had their logistics expert offer ideas on how the retailer could enhance their efficiency—suggestions that were completely unrelated to pallets. According to CHEP's president, Rex Lowe, "We believe this special gift of CHEP's to the prospect helped us land a multimillion dollar contract."

Use Informational Follow-Up

Service research tells us that few actions enhance the devotion of customers more than simple follow-up. When a customer makes a major purchase, most likely the salesperson can help dispel "buyer's remorse" with a cheery "How's it working for you?" phone call, including some affirming statement about the customer's brilliance in recognizing value!

Follow-up also can be a major tool to enhance learning for your customers. A hotel's reputation for good service can be boosted if the front desk person who checked you in calls a bit later to learn whether you're satisfied with the room. Magnetic service providers go one step further and use the brief call to point out a room feature, leaving the customer wiser. Devotion can soar with one-line tutoring statements like: "I just wanted to remind you that your desk chair is adjustable," or "Let us know if we can bring a fax machine to your room," or "The high speed Internet connection is inside the desk drawer, on the right."

A group of physicians went on the aggressive to ensure that their patients were health wise. Patients were asked how they preferred their physician to send them follow-up information. Many opted for mail. However, a large number opted for e-mail with attachments, or fax.

Within 24 hours after every visit, physicians now send information to patients in the fashion designated. Articles are included that relate to the patient's condition. A health maintenance newsletter is also sent quarterly with information on how to remain healthy.

The training company mentioned earlier departed from the traditional approach of loading up participants with giant course notebooks. Instead, they parceled out some of the information after the learning experience. They also put their participants on an e-mail list so that they would receive periodic learning material to help bolster their learning and retention.

. . .

We live in chaotic times. Massive changes are making life seem like a roller coaster that has gone out of control. While we may enjoy a certain amount of diversity and newness, too much can leave us overwhelmed and troubled. We worry about getting behind and not being able to change fast enough. And "becoming obsolete," both professionally and personally, threatens our livelihood and our lives. The antidote is learning, constant learning. W. Edwards Deming put his finger on it when he wrote: "Learning is not compulsory—neither is survival."

Helping customers stay ahead of the curve doesn't have to feel like a compulsory, survival-of-the-fittest proposition. It can be an engaging and edifying experience—even fun. "Just a spoonful of sugar makes the medicine go down" says the popular song from the movie *Mary Poppins*. It communicates a philosophy long used by smart parents with cranky kids, and clever teachers with reluctant pupils. This does not mean that the rules of curiosity engagement are of the parent-child, teacher-student variety. It means that when we make learning a delightful addition to the service experience, we create an experience that increases customer devotion.

. . .

If you want to build a ship, don't drum up people together to collect wood and don't assign them tasks and work, but rather teach them to long for the endless immensity of the sea."
—Antoine de Saint-Exupery

Secret #5

Give Customers an Occasional Miracle

magnetism A magnetic field cannot be seen with the naked eye; however, its pull can be felt and observed through its works.

magnetic service Magnetic service is unexpected. It comes from a deep understanding of what customers value, which service providers learn by invisible means but demonstrate in surprising ways.

A Boston family adopted an Asian girl. No sooner had she arrived in the United States than the family learned she needed to have surgery. The nine-year-old child—who spoke only Chinese and whose life experiences were limited to those she had encountered in a small Chinese village and in her trip to the United States—was noticeably anxious.

Her surgery was fortunately successful. As she was about to be discharged, she was asked through an interpreter, "What most surprised you about your stay here at Children's Memorial Hospital of Boston?" The child smiled and proudly responded, "I did not know my doctor would be Chinese."

The Meaning of Miracle Power

Delight your customer! Exceed your customers' expectations! Provide value-added service! These have been the mantras of customer-service gurus for a long time. Such focus on "adding more" has raised the quality of service in many organizations. It has also raised customers' standards for what qualifies as "good service."

But what's an organization to do when the budget-cutting ax is loosed and tight profit margins get even tighter? How do leaders avoid sending a very mixed message by telling the front line to wow their customers in the morning and announcing staff cutbacks and expense reductions in the afternoon? How can you add value when there are no more resources to fund extra added attractions? In a phrase: Offer the occasional miracle!

Producing the occasional miracle is different from exceeding customer expectations. Ask customers what actions would be value added in a given situation and they will focus on those that take the expected experience to a higher level—meaning those that make them walk away feeling "they gave me *more* than I anticipated." Value added is the upgrade, the extra helping, the complimentary dessert. It is a linear extension of good service.

What makes a service miracle a miracle is the fact that it is unpredictable. An example might make clearer the distinction between the simple delight caused by a courtesy upgrade and the enchantment provoked by the occasional miracle.

A couple bought a new house in an upper-middle class neighborhood. Neither enjoyed yard work so they talked with the neighbors about the "caretaker of choice." "You have to hire Bill," was the line most heard in the couple's "find a gardener" search. So, Bill was summoned to their house late one afternoon for an "audition."

Bill arrived in an old pickup truck loaded with garden equipment.

Dressed in faded jeans, a "gimme" tee-shirt from Miracle Gro®, and a sweat-stained cowboy hat, he leaped out of the front seat. Grabbing a stack of pale green index cards and a pencil, he literally ran up the sidewalk to ring the doorbell. "These caladiums are getting too much water," he announced even before introducing himself to the owners at the front door.

Once invited in, Bill removed his boots and hat, leaving them on the front steps. Inside, he confidently began his inquisition and completed his index cards. He acted as if he had already been hired and was there to complete his "know your customer" records. His eyes scanned the living room like those of a police officer at a crime scene. The couple's initial reservations quickly give way to confidence as this straight-talking, no-nonsense gardener was getting poised to show off "professionalism in progress."

His questions were as rapid fire as his gait. "What time do you get home from work? Do you mind if the sidewalk is wet when you get home? What's your favorite color? Do you ever pick flowers from your yard to use inside? How do you want me to communicate with you? What do you folks do for fun on the weekend? When you go fishing, what do you like to catch? Do you have pets you let outdoors? What do you like least about your yard? Whose yard in this neighborhood do you most admire? Can I have another glass of iced tea?"

On Bill's first "every Thursday" yard cutting, the owners left for work early that morning and returned late that afternoon to find the yard immaculate. A pale green index card left in the mail box—the agreed-upon spot for written communication—had one line written in pencil: "I moved that Foster holly to a shadier spot, no charge—Bill." The next week there was no note, just an article torn out of a gardening magazine about chemical-free fertilizer.

Then, a small service miracle happened.

It was the week Bill was replacing the annuals in the front yard. The couple had agreed that Bill would replace the summer geraniums with pansies for the winter. The couple came home on Thursday to find the usual immaculate yard plus a front flower bed filled with pansies. They went to the mail box to see what message Bill had left. Inside was the signature pale green index card with a note that read: "Go look under the big oak tree on top of the concrete block." Racing to the back yard they found a large Styrofoam® cup of earthworms in moist soil. On the cup Bill had penciled, "Hope you all catch a big one this weekend." Bill had remembered that they were avid fishermen and provided a "value unique" gesture that left them enchanted.

Keep the Miracle Small

The magnetism of the occasional miracle is in part due to its size. Red carpet and limousines may be great for a rock star in need of an ego boost. But such extravagance makes the typical customer embarrassed and unnecessarily indebted for the gesture. A simple gesture says, "I care;" an opulent one says, "You owe me." The goal is to create an unexpected, unpredictable positive encounter that becomes the fodder for "you're not going to believe this" stories that customers tell their friends.

A couple on their first Celebrity cruise found the proverbial fruit basket in their cabin upon boarding. Wanting to get in some last-minute dockside shopping before the ship got under way, the couple quickly unpacked their belongings and left their cabin without touching the fruit basket on the table. When they arrived a couple of hours later they were moved to discover that the housekeeper had left two small plates and a dinner knife beside the fruit basket. A missing item? Not according to these devoted customers. After their fifth cruise with Celebrity, they still talk about the tiny but thoughtful gesture that warmed their hearts on their first cruise.

The Nicholson-Hardie clerks had always been smart and friendly—just like those of their competitors. The well-lit store in a convenient up-scale shopping area had always been overstocked with a wide variety of green plants, garden hoses, clay pots, and such—just like those of their competitors. They became the talk of the town, though, when they added two big cats that took turns sleeping on the checkout counter. Appropriately named Nick and Hardie, the cats even had busi-ness cards displayed in a card holder on the counter that proclaimed their job title—store cat. Mention Nicholson-Hardie to a local and you are likely to get "That's the garden store with the cats."

The key takeaway is not to take a copycat (sorry about that) approach and add a cat to make a customer-service miracle. Many retail department stores a few years ago foolishly added a grand piano and piano player to mimic successful Seattle-based Nordstrom. Unfortunately, it was not the piano that made Nordstrom successful. The signature piano simply symbolized an assemblage of practices that created a memorable service experience that was unique to the store. The same goes for Nicholson-Hardie with their cats. "We were looking for a particular tone and feel to our store," says co-president Josh Bracken, "and the cats were part of an assortment of things that would help accomplish that."

Look for Miracle Making in the Outcome after the Outcome

Kim Burke of Avalon Salon in Dallas has been a hairstylist for men and women for several years. Doing far more than what the old-fashioned barbers of yesteryear did, Kim gives her customers a shampoo, scalp massage, awesome tea, and conversation laced with more culture than chitchat. But Kim sometimes adds a twist to her customer's hair care—she offers a second shampoo and blow dry after she finishes a haircut. Instead of the customer's last memory being an irritating itch on the back of the neck, he or she leaves knowing that Kim understands that the real outcome is not hair that has been correctly cut, but customers *feeling good* when checking out her artistry in the rear-view mirror.

Kim asked several of her best customers, "When you think about this haircut 24 hours from now, what most concerns you?" When several of her customers mentioned "trying to make it look like it does when you finish here," she gave them a hand mirror and turned them so that customers could watch what she was doing in the large mirror. As she styled a customer's hair, she also demonstrated and described ways to replicate her techniques.

Magnetic service providers consider "the outcome beyond the outcome." This means thinking about what the customer will be doing with the service or outcome after you have done what the customer expected. For example, if you are a car sales person, your customer's expected outcome might be purchasing a car. You might consider your selling role as pretty much being over when you see the taillights leaving the lot. You might think, "Well, I've done my part, it's up to the folks in the service department when the customer returns for maintenance or repair for the rest." But what if you thought about the customer's next outcome (arriving home with a brand new car) and staged a welcome celebration with balloons and banners? That's the small miracle, considering the outcome beyond the expected outcome.

Nordstrom is famous for pursuing the outcome beyond the outcome approach. "We try to guess what is beyond the customer's purchase," says John McClesky of the men's suits department at the Dallas store. "If a customer buys a sports jacket, the obvious extension might be to sell him slacks or a tie. But if you learn that the customer is buying the jacket for a cruise, you might explore dressy shorts, an ascot, or a Panama hat." John continues: "And slipping a complimentary set of collar stays in the newly purchased jacket pocket (a frequently forgotten item on a trip) can leave a customer absolutely awed."

Play out in your mind the possibilities of what customers will be doing, thinking, and feeling after you have met their presented need. What small gesture would make this customer swoon? Sometimes a bit of subtle conversation about life after the purchase can reveal opportunities. Instead of asking, "How do you plan to use your new camera?" ask, "What will you do with it in the next week or so?" Instead of asking, "Would there be anything else?" ask, "What have we not thought of that would make your hotel stay really special?" Make your queries reach into the future, and the customer will provide you with clues as to how you can produce the unexpected occasional miracle.

Make Miracles with What You Don't Do

We generally think of a magnetic service experience as involving something unique that the service provider does. Sometimes, though, the special moment can come from what is not done.

Grey Dog Trading Company in Tucson, Arizona, is a dealer in Native American art, mostly from the Southwest. Owners Kent and Laurie McManus particularly enjoy customers who come and spend hours examining rugs, pottery, and paintings. A visit might include a sit-down coffee with Kent or Laurie and a long discussion about trends in

Indian art. The sales aspect has been completely removed from the experience. What's left is customers experiencing the miracle of people loving their product and wanting to share their passion with others.

What stands out in your own service encounters that, if removed or hidden, might make the experience more miraculous? The San Diego Zoo's Wild Animal Park outside of Escondido, California, gives visitors a relatively "up close and personal" experience of animals from the wild. In charting a glassed-in train ride through the zoo, the designers avoided creating a smooth, predictable trip. Instead the rail car takes unexpected turns, making the encounter with wildlife more realistic and exciting. "If you see you are approaching a giraffe, you have time to mentally prepare," explained the tour guide. "But if you take a sharp turn and are suddenly eyeball level with one, it is much more real and certainly more memorable."

Make Miracles Out of Your Generosity

Customers like to be reminded from time to time of our gratitude for their patronage. If we fail to thank them they will come to assume they are being taken for granted. Expressions of generosity can be a powerful source of miracle making.

Chanaka Demel, the front desk clerk at the Holiday Inn Select hotel at the Toronto Airport, was registering two men late one evening. As he was checking them in, one guest communicated his anger over the fact that the airline had lost their luggage. Both men were scheduled for important early morning interviews and now lacked the proper clothes. Realizing that both guests were about his size, he signaled another clerk to fill in for him and went home to secure two suits, two shirts, and all of the appropriate accessories for the guests. They returned to the hotel late the next day after completing a successful day of interviews in Chanaka's clothes. "He's a miracle worker," the men told the general manager. "We plan to tell everyone to stay at this hotel in the future."

On his way out of town, Bilijack stopped in Lenox Square Rich's in Atlanta to purchase a suit that had just gone on sale for a trip he was making. Sensing that Bilijack was in a hurry, the sales person, Michael Gruber, asked him to watch the men's department while he ran to the other side of the store to get a tailor. The tailor dropped everything, measured Bilijack, and had the suit altered in twenty minutes. Feeling great about the purchase and the generous service, Bilijack elected to purchase a second suit before leaving for his trip!

Miracle Making in Action

Offering the occasional service miracle has many advantages. Organizations that promote a perpetual "exceeding customer expectations" approach can leave the front line in search of ever more costly gestures to keep the standards climbing. Champagne treatment today becomes helicopters tomorrow. At some point the organization runs out of room to one-up the last experience, while the budget is left empty. Occasional miracle making gets you out of this rut.

The occasional service miracle has another advantage. As do those who plan a surprise birthday party, the creators gain as much as the recipients. The pursuit of an occasional miracle helps service providers think differently about customers. Connections are more personal; communications more attentive. It also causes them to think creatively about every aspect of their role, not just those related to serving the customer. Finally, when people are a part of a culture that strives for customer enchantment, there is a greater sense of joy and passion conferred on customers, who, in turn, reciprocate with their gratitude and loyalty.

• • •

This is the era of the short term. We expect results to happen faster and faster and faster. The taxi does not go fast enough, the stock market is not open long enough, the sales graph does not rise steeply enough, quickly enough. The frenetic raising of all standards creates a greed mentality. "How can I help?" has been too often replaced with "What have you done for me lately?" We think far more about squeezing margins than we do about offering extra helpings.

Customers are devoted to service providers that are not preoccupied with keeping score. Magnetic service providers know that generosity works like love; the more you give the more there is. The "giver" mentality is what makes marriages work, partnerships prosper, and customers stay enchanted.

Yet, offering daily dazzlement can become a dead-end and too familiar street. If we brought our loved one flowers every single day, sooner or later the gesture would be seen as less and less captivating. However, continually looking for the opportunity to produce the once-in-a-while surprise creates an invisible force that elicits customer devotion. And there are few things in the world of enterprise more affirming, rewarding, and exciting than having customers unwaveringly drawn to your product or service.

• • •

"Breakthroughs come from an instinctive judgment of what customers might want if they knew to think about it."
—Andrew Grove, CEO, Intel

Secret #6

Empower Customers Through Comfort

magnetism Magnetic force causes individual and random items to align in the direction of the magnetic field.

magnetic service Magnetic service is steady. It leaves customers with a sense of power or security due to the fact that the varied and diverse units that customers must encounter are aligned and in sync in ways that are consistent and comfortable to customers.

"Charlie's not doing well," Ed's wife said on the phone as he was fighting homebound traffic late on a Friday afternoon. "He's probably not going to live through the weekend." Charlie had been suffering a four-year bout with cancer. The remission had lasted a year . . . and then the cancer returned with a vengeance. Ed had been expecting this kind of call for a few weeks.

His wife continued. "Why don't you stop by the grocery store and pick up a large deli tray we can take to the family sometime tomorrow?" In that region of the country, food was always a helpful antidote to sorrow. Ed pulled into a very large grocery store and made his way past the floral department and auto repair center to the clerk behind the meat counter of the well-stocked delicatessen section.

"I'd like a large deli tray," Ed explained to the deli clerk, fully expecting a "coming right up" response.

"I'm sorry, but we're out of deli trays," the clerk said, without expression or eye contact.

"Oh, that's okay," Ed responded. "I'll just shop around the store, pick up a few items I know we need, and give you a chance to make one up."

"Nope," the clerk replied, still sporting a monotone attitude. "The woman who makes the deli trays has already gone." Ed wondered what had made this task such a specialized skill. He had visions of the absent worker at the Deli Tray Makers Convention in Las Vegas. But he didn't want to go home empty-handed. He'd simply purchase all the makings for a deli tray and his wife could assemble it. "Okay, then I'd like a half-pound each of ham, turkey, and roast beef sliced thin."

As the clerk put all the items on the counter, price-marked for checkout, Ed made one more attempt to thaw her icy disposition. "How much would you charge me for one of those plastic trays with a lid on it?"

"You can't buy a tray unless you buy a tray," was her lifeless response.

"I beg your pardon?" Ed queried, not trusting his ears. This time her bored look was accompanied by a tone like a hostile arrow—pointed and belligerent. "I *said* you can't get a tray unless you get a tray!"

What Ed had encountered was a makeshift inventory system. At the end of the day, the clerk counted the number of empty trays left from the morning's supply to determine how many deli trays had been sold. No tray unless Ed was willing to pay the fully loaded price. Ed left feeling affronted by the clerk's newfound aggression and beaten down by a senseless system—an unhappy, uncomfortable, and "disempowered" customer.

So, What's an Empowered Customer?

"Empowerment" is a word usually applied to employees. Being empowered means having the responsible freedom to effectively respond to any situation. But what does empowerment mean on the customer side of the equation? And where does it fit in with magnetic service?

Customers enjoy having a sense of security and predictability in the service they receive. Granted, we all like an occasional positive surprise, but the core parts of the service must above all signal reliability. An empowered customer is one who feels an internal sense of power in the service experience—a sense of being in control and secure, not off balance.

Customers feel empowered when they feel psychologically comfortable. They experience this with organizations that offer their value proposition in unmistakable terms, that communicate clear expectations, and that consistently deliver on what they promise. Customers look for cues and clues that tell them they will be secure in their dealings with you and your organization.

Customers also feel empowered when they are physically comfortable. "Comfortable" is a much bigger concept than "easy," as in, "easy to do business with." "Easy" has the connotation of simple and effortless. "Comfortable" carries the more involved notion of being free of anxiety. Customers are quite willing for your service to be complex and to require some effort to obtain. They are often willing to work for what they get. In fact, stripping complexity from service risks rendering it sterile and lifeless; eliminating all effort may lower its value in the eyes of the customer (think five-star restaurant as accessible as a fast-food restaurant). What you are after is a reasonable match between effort and payoff—and an experience that, though complex, makes sense.

Purposeless Processes Create Defensive Aggression

Service happens through an experience—a process that the service provider uses to link "customer need" to "customer need met." Sometimes the processes are simple and short; sometimes they are involved and complex. Processes are an integral part of the service encounter and cannot be eliminated.

All service processes are created for a reason. No one comes to work thinking: How can I install a pointless process that will make it more difficult for customers to get what they want? Many processes are installed almost solely for the benefit of the service provider (think about the typical hospital admission procedure). Some are crafted to ease the customers' anxiety (think of a comfortable waiting area of an automobile dealership). And some help both customer and server.

Sometimes the rationale for the process disappears. In a perfect world, the service process would self-destruct when it was no longer required. Unfortunately, most remain. And irrelevant service processes are a greater liability to the organization than bad service processes. When a process has no real purpose, it requires a more ardent defense. As customers challenge the irrelevant process, the service worker (a.k.a. the process guardian) feels compelled to take steps to protect it. As the process becomes even more irrelevant, the guardian becomes even more belligerent. Unfortunately, customers get more strident in their attack, as well.

Take a trip down memory lane. Recall the last time you visited the Department of Motor Vehicles, rented a car at an airport, filed an insurance claim, purchased food at the grocery store at a peak time, or contacted your local cable company. You probably thought to yourself: I know I could completely reinvent this process to be more customer friendly.

The truth is you probably could. But the guardians of archaic processes that don't have any real or obvious purpose feel compelled to shield the process from being overhauled or improved. Try suggesting an improvement and you will get an earful of why it HAS to be the way it is, coupled with "You don't understand how we do business here." And, like Ed's deli clerk, they habitually cope with inane bureaucracy and pointless red tape by assuming a robotic stance completely devoid of authentic connection or enthusiasm.

A Quick Story to Provide the Reason

The story that follows about gorillas is a rubric that has been around for a while. It is compelling because we've all witnessed variations on its theme in our encounters with organizations or units. While we are not gorillas, we become victim to the same blindness when behaviors are learned for a reason and then the reason disappears.

An experiment was conducted with four gorillas who were moved into the same cage. When the gorillas were first introduced into the environment, the experimenters lowered bananas into the center of the cage. When the gorillas went after the food, all four were hosed down with a high-pressure water hose. Even if only one went after the food, all received the same treatment. As expected, soon the gorillas did not go after the bananas when they were lowered into the cage. Then the experimenters stopped using the hose and replaced one of the gorillas.

When the bananas were lowered into the cage, the new gorilla, of course, started toward the free meal. The other three gorillas knew what would happen, so they quickly jumped the new gorilla, keeping him from causing the dreaded gush of water. Although perplexed, the new gorilla quickly learned not to go after the food lowered into the cage, and to jump any other gorilla that did the same.

The experimenters continued by slowly replacing each gorilla one by one. The result was the same: The new one went for the food, and the others jumped him. Soon the experimenters had replaced all of the four original gorillas. Keep in mind that the high-pressure water hose had not been used since the first four gorillas were together. But every time a new gorilla went for the food lowered into the cage, the others stopped him cold. The experimenters were able to go several genera-tions away from the original four gorillas, but still the behavior did not change. None of the gorillas knew why they shouldn't go for the food, but they knew they'd get jumped on if they did. And none of them knew why they were jumping other gorillas if they went for the food. It was simply what had been done before them, and before them, and before them. A proud tradition had been born.

Raising the Comfort Quotient

How do you get "the new gorillas to go for the bananas?" How do you get the deli tray clerk to put Ed's simple request above an archaic approach to inventory management? What does it take to see irrelevant processes so that they can be reinvented or dismantled and replaced so that your service offers more customer comfort and empowerment?

Look for Where Energy Is Expended Illogically

One technique for seeing irrational processes is to look for places where people seem to be spending abnormal or illogical amounts of energy defending, shoring up, patching, explaining, or managing. "He doth protest too much," wrote Shakespeare in *Julius Caesar*. Places in the organization that "protest too much" are crying out for examination and repair. Which departments seem to have the highest turnover? What procedures seem to be the most frequent cause of delay? What topics most frequently dominate the agenda of management?

"Sometimes it reminds me of a kind of emotional Geiger counter," says Shannon Brennan, VP for customer service for AvalonBay Communities, a company headquartered in Alexandria, Virginia, that builds and manages luxury apartment communities around the country. "We have lots of ways for customers to give us honest feedback. You can read through comment cards, review a customer survey, or sit in on one of our many focus groups. You can also learn a lot by listening to the resident issues our community managers raise—the intensity as well as the frequency. We have front-line people who are terrific at acting as a conduit between residents and the company. Just follow their emotional Geiger counter and it will lead you directly to what residents rave about as well as what they rant about."

Interview New People about "How We Do Things around Here"

It takes about ninety days to go blind to the details customers see. As we get acclimated, oriented, and inculcated into a new culture, those illogical processes—the ones people are talking about when they say, "That's just the way we do things here"—fade away. We stop seeing what seemed obvious initially. This means new people are more able to see that the "Emperor is not wearing any clothes." And people in magnetic service organizations seek them out and tap their perception like anthropologists in search of an explanation.

Sewell GMC in Dallas is well known for making the car-buying, trading, or service process super comfortable. "We work hard to get honest feedback from our customers," says long-time salesman Rick McIntire. "We also know our new employees can spot stuff our veteran employees might take for granted. A part of the 'getting on board' orientation is to have new people tell us what we do that seems unnecessary or uncomfortable for customers."

Appoint a bureaucracy-busting team to question every rule or procedure in the organization. Better yet, try "zero-based restriction". Zero-based budgeting says that rather than taking last year's budget and adding a certain percentage to it, you build each year's budget from scratch—allowing you to take nothing for granted. Zero-based restriction therefore suggests you throw out all the restrictions and add back only the ones that are necessary. Again, the discipline enables you to take nothing for granted in inspecting the relevance of some sacred cows that may have outlived their purpose.

Let Complaint Frequency Point to Improvement Opportunities

If you asked every front-line employee to note the target of customers' ire, you would discover that some processes get more negative attention from customers than others. Let this complaint frequency instruct you. Fix first what customers say is the biggest headache. Then put people to work finding routes to improve on the next biggest, and the next, and the next.

Milwaukee-based Aurora Health Care's appointment schedulers in some of the smaller clinics often had other duties that took them away from the appointment desk. Customers complained that when they called to schedule an appointment, they frequently would get an answering machine. Once the irritant was discovered, a group of schedulers from various clinics found a way to fix the problem—schedulers were given remote phones allowing them to answer the phone no matter where they were in the clinic.

Get Customers and Vendors to Help You Troubleshoot Processes

When John Longstreet (currently SVP with ClubCorp) was the general manager of the Harvey Hotel in Plano, Texas, he had a practice of soliciting unique help from frequent guests. In exchange for a free meal (sans wine) in the hotel restaurant or a complimentary room on a weekend night, he had the guest come to his office after checking in. He gave the guest a set of special tasks that only John knew about. The guest was to follow the task instructions and at the end of his or her stay to complete a detailed feedback sheet outlining what happened.

The instructions ranged from the unusual ("Call for room service at 3 a.m.") to the extreme ("Call the front desk and request fifteen bath towels") to the bizarre ("Deliberately break a glass in the restaurant"). The guest was to report how the situations were handled so that the Harvey could surface (and hopefully eliminate) those components of the process that resulted in a negative experience for guests.

John also used vendors, suppliers, and others to unearth ineffective processes. For example, he held focus group sessions with the cab drivers who most often brought guests to and from the hotel property. "Guests will tell us they had a good experience when they are checking out. But they sometimes tell a different story to the cab driver who is transporting them to the airport after their stay," John says. "We encourage the cab drivers we know to be our ears for disgruntled guests. It enables us to zero in on something we think is working but is an irritant to guests."

Frosty Acres is a large wholesale food distributor headquartered in Alpharetta, Georgia. Their annual customer meeting includes vendors and other business partners as well as customers. "We see these meetings as a way to showcase what we can do for our partners," says CEO George Watson. "But, selfishly, it is a way for us to get feedback about what gets in the way of our giving great service. If we create the right setting and ask the right questions, we can learn a lot about what we need to improve to make doing business with Frosty Acres a heck of a lot easier."

Pay Attention When Customers Emote Stories Rather than Relate Facts

One of the best cues that lets you know you have stumbled onto a purposeless process is an irate customer who insists on bending your ear to hear his or her story rather than simply telling you the facts. There is a vast difference between "My new dryer stopped heating up and I need someone to come fix it" and "Let me tell you what happened . . . I called your company and your hateful receptionist told me . . . ."

Anger is not always irrational. People can be very upset and completely rational. "Upset and rational" is generally born of a service breakdown that made sense, meaning it was unacceptable but explainable, unsatisfactory but understandable. However, let the customer be the victim of a process that makes no sense and you get a completely different level of emotion. The customer is driven to tell you the story not just to get you to repair a busted experience, but to make you see the ludicrousness of the experience. While it is easy to take such responses personally, it is helpful to remember that sometimes the customer's goal is to do more than gain your empathy so you will be bold in your solution, but to punish you (as a representative of your organization) by making you see what an idiot you are (or your process is).

Get a Nearby Unit to Critique Your Service

A friend of ours was staying at the historical Brown Palace Hotel in Denver while working there for a week. On Friday morning, as he was checking out, he remarked to the desk clerk, "Can you give me really clear directions on how to get from the hotel to Denver International Airport? I have a rental car and don't know the city very well."

"I can do better than that," the desk clerk replied with a smile in her voice as grand as the one on her face. "I can give you this!" She presented the guest with a 3 x 5 note card with detailed instructions for driving from the hotel to the airport.

"This is great!" our friend remarked. "I stay in a lot of hotels and no one has ever given me a helpful tool like this."

"You want to know who came up with this idea?" she asked play-fully. And before he could respond she blurted out: "The guys at the bell stand! Before we had these cards we'd send you to the bell stand for driving directions since they drive the hotel van. But sometimes they were tied up helping guests with luggage. They suggested we put answers to the most frequently asked guest questions on small cards. And it's worked terrifically. It makes them more accessible and it makes us look smarter."

"Oh, you mean you have others like this?" our friend continued, somewhat in awe. "Oh, yes!" she replied with great pleasure, as she pulled out a stack of different colored cards. "Where would you like to go?"

Units who work around us can often see service obstacles we miss. Like employees at the bell stand, they are often entangled in our purposeless processes. Simply by inviting these other units to provide friendly critique can help make a process in need of transformation more obvious.

Reward Boundary Hunters

Chuck Salter, CEO of Commerce Bank in Cherry Hill, New Jersey, trans-formed a thirty-year-old traditional bank into a "world-class service" bank. From 1990 to 2000, profits rose 2,000%—all from his thinking like a retailer, not like a banker. Just as Nordstrom has "Nordies" (their term for devoted customers), Commerce Bank has its "Wow Team." There are Wow Awards, a VP of Wow, and a Wow Department. Realiz-ing that a cultural makeover would require new processes, Salter insti-tuted a "Kill a Stupid Rule" program. Any employee who spots a rule that keeps employees from wowing customers gets a fifty-dollar reward.

Certain processes and procedures can create artificial boundaries between elements of your organization that should be functioning together, seamlessly and openly. These are the kind of boundaries that need to be hunted down and eliminated. Put everyone on notice to spot purposeless processes and illogical boundaries. Hold gatherings for people to report their findings. Make busting bureaucracy more valued than protecting those sacred cows in need of being put out to pasture.

Making service comfortable is all about making the customer's experience calm and secure, and being accessible (so that customers can reach the organization easily and when they want to). Customers of Cox's Dry Cleaners in Dallas know that comfort starts with owner Sam Cox. He was one of the first in the dry cleaning business to put both an after-hours keyed drop box in the front of the store and a drive-in pickup service in the back. If you need to get your clothes on Sunday when Sam is normally closed, regulars know that a call to Sam at home will get him there in a heartbeat.

Customers today have a low tolerance for being hassled. While they do not expect perfection all the time, they are devoted to organizations that consistently demonstrate a commitment to taking the kinks and toils out of the process of getting service. Providing service comfort requires vigilance as well as caretaking. It calls for people who are willing to raise their hand when they spot customer discomfort, frustration, or insecurity. It takes people who see continuous process improvement as vital as continuous revenue improvement. And it requires people who make preventive maintenance an integral part of their stewardship of the organization's resources and reputation.

• • •

"Few things help an individual more than to place responsibility upon him, and to let him know you trust him."
—Booker T. Washington

Secret #7

Reveal Your Character by Unveiling Your Courage

magnetism A magnet is the substance of a compass that enables the user to locate true North.

magnetic service Magnetic service is upright. It discloses to the customer that the service has substance, that it is grounded in a set of core values gallantly honored by the service provider.

Marty Davidson, chairman of Southern Pipe & Supply (an independent wholesale distributor of plumbing supplies headquartered in Meridian, Mississippi) has built a loyal and growing customer base of builders and contractors through his company's commitment to service. One day several years ago, Davidson received a call from a customer complaining that a $2.50 part had been left out of his shipment. The customer was in southern Louisiana and would have to keep a crew idle until the part arrived. It was too late for overnight delivery.

Without hesitation, Davidson put the part into the hands of an employee and got the employee on the next plane to New Orleans, where he delivered the part and then stayed overnight before returning home.

Was Davidson driven by some official service guarantee or legal obligation? Nope. What was the cost to Southern Pipe & Supply? More than $1000. What possessed Davidson to take what any cost accountant would see as a foolish move? The answer lies not in the fanatical customer devotion and word-of-mouth marketing that occurred as a result of Davidson's decision—those were the happy consequences. The answer lies in his character.

"I have learned one thing that has made my business a success," says Davidson. "You cannot live your values only during the good times. The real test is to live them during the bad times. Besides, the $2.50 part incident was a good way to remind everyone in my shop about what is really important around here."

The Colors of Character Revealed

"Character" is one of those vibrant words that can be used to paint many colorful word pictures. Webster's really big dictionary has twenty-eight definitions! The word is derived from the Greek word "engraved." It is the antithesis of the "morality for the moment." It instead connotes solidity, constancy, and permanence.

We view the Enron-WorldCom-Tyco scandals as offenses perpetrated by leaders whose character was shifty and acquiescent rather than grounded and steadfast. Enron-type scandals aren't created by greedy leaders. They are created by spineless leaders who are reluctant to stand up for character, preferring to sit still for consent. Sure, in these cases there is greed. But there is a lot more acquiescence than avarice—way too many middle managers who quietly and privately tell their spouses what they should have loudly and publicly told their bosses and colleagues.

One of the world's leading distributors of after-market motorcycle and power sports vehicles is Fort Worth, Texas-based Tucker-Rocky

Distributing. The company made a decision to consolidate from twelve U.S. distribution centers down to eight larger and more intelligent centers. Such a move was not remarkable in business, particularly since the original twelve centers had evolved through acquisitions and therefore lacked consistent standards and up-to-date technology. What was unique was the manner in which President Frank Esposito elected to communicate the decision to the marketplace.

"There will likely be many rumors and rampant speculation," Esposito said in a telephone conference with the media. "However, please accept my promise that I have just given you all of the facts as they are known today. This is the total package of information—complete and honest." The coverage in the industry media was supportive and accurate. The media knew the character of Tucker-Rocky. If Frank said it was so, you could take it to the bank.

"Character" also means someone who is odd or unusual. A "character" in the traditional view of organizational life is an entity to be shunned. When someone labels someone "a real character," the tag borders on pejorative. It implies maverick, eccentric—even weirdo. The truth is, great organizations and great units are spawned by great characters. Breakthroughs and record-bustings are generally done by characters . . . those wild ducks who courageously march (fly?) to their own drum.

Talk to anyone who's done something really interesting in the marketplace—Turner Broadcasting, Dell Computer, Schwab, Amazon.com, and you'll find someone who was labeled "crazy" or "insane" by pundits, analysts, academics, and competitors. Talk to anyone who's done something really interesting and provocative within an organization, and you'll find someone labeled "weird" or "loony." These are "characters" in the purest sense of the word: individuals focused on creating and growing something new, something distinctive, something their customers will be unwaveringly drawn to.

Characters with character focus on improving, creating, shaping—not on destroying others or enhancing their self-image at someone else's expense. Character breeds focus and honesty. Political gamesmanship, deception, and weasel tactics are simply clutter. There's no need or time for them. There's too much cool stuff to be done. Accordingly, they sometimes threaten people with their strength, foresight, and commitment. They're also the ones who get things done and build new value.

Showing Your Colors

Customers adore character—the solid "engraved with honesty and integrity" side, as well as the maverick side. Most customers feel much more confident dealing with service providers who are likely to remain on the scene. And customers believe that goodness will win out over shadiness and that innovators will last longer than "me-too'ers."

How do you unite all the aspects of character to not only produce magnetic service but also in the process show customers how you intend to stay connected with them over the long haul? We have studied the "lives" of organizations that not only thrive but endure. Researcher Arie de Geus found that the average life expectancy of a multinational corporation—*Fortune* 500 Company or its equivalent—is forty to fifty years. Forty percent of newly created companies last less than ten years. Yet, there are some that last centuries (Royal Dutch/Shell, W.R. Grace, DuPont, Rolls Royce, Kodak, Suzuki, etc.). De Geus studied the companies that had lasted many years to learn what they had in common. First among the four commonalities included a strong and enduring sense of purpose.

Help Customers See You Are Clear About Who You Are

"Committed to helping men dress better than they have to." These words are the tag line of a radio ad for Pockets Men's Wear in Dallas. We needed to find out whether their methods matched their moniker. And we got our socks knocked off.

Pockets was founded over twenty-five years ago by David Smith, a twenty-six-year-old veteran of a men's wear chain. Appalled by the mediocre way business professionals dressed for work, he opened his own store to pursue a dream of making men's fashion matter—and matter deeply—to lawyers, bankers, and other professionals. His goal was for his salespeople to be fashion consultants and clothing mentors to their customers. He also knew that the only way to get people "back in his store/school" was through magnetic service.

The ambiance of the store is most definitely that of a store on a mission. The merchandise is *GQ* cover material. The setting is sophisticated but warmly comfortable. Salespeople have a perfect blend of folksy and classy making them seem confidently elegant, with every bit of the arrogance removed! These same people give seminars to professional associations on how to dress for achievement . The fact that they have several tailors standing by assures customers that their unique requirements will be met in a hurry.

Doug Duckworth, a salesman with Pockets for over twenty-five years, puts it this way: "We want people to come in because of the great men's wear they expect; we want them to come back because of the great service they don't expect." David Smith was a pioneer in the "no restrictions" return policy. "Sure, I get ripped off once in a while," said Smith. "But trust only comes to you when you're willing to show it to others. I know I would want others to treat me that way."

Another sixteen-year veteran, salesperson Sharon Kuhl, proudly relates the service heroics that have become their trademark—like the ones that came into play for the guy who spilled salad dressing on his shirt at lunch right before the BIG meeting. "We had a replacement to him in minutes," she says. Smith adds the story of the out-of-towner whose pants cuff had come unraveled. "We had the tailor repair it and press it, and had the customer quickly out the door—no charge. That customer now flies back to Dallas solely to buy clothes at Pockets."

"We have no plans to open a chain or franchise," says Smith. "It would dilute the purity of our mission and the uniqueness of what we do. We want to produce the smartest, best-dressed businessman in the office as well as on the golf course. We've done our job when our customers dress better than they have to . . . because they have caught our passion and love for great fashion."

Pockets vision is what you see working the sales floor, not what you read hanging on the wall!

Boldly Follow Your Vision

The publisher of this book—Berrett-Koehler Publishers—is renowned for courageously following a vision. In the 1980s and early 90s, Steve Piersanti headed the Business and Higher Education Division of Jossey-

Bass Publishers. By 1991, the economy (as well as the publisher) was struggling. However, Steve's division was the only one operating with a profit. When Jossey-Bass was purchased by media mogul Robert Maxwell, Steve hoped this would be an opportunity to add staff to respond to the growing demand for books from his division.

Maxwell had other plans. Famous for his ruthless turnaround tactics and "slash and burn" approach to expense reduction, he put out a directive that every department was to cut staff by 15 percent. The idea of cutting people who had worked hard to create a profitable division seemed wrong to Steve. He requested that his division be exempt. The pithy answer from New York was the equivalent of George Bush Senior's "Read my lips." Steve was not giving up. He flew to New York to meet with Maxwell while Maxwell was staying at the Waldorf Astoria and pleaded his case. The meeting lasted seconds; the order stood and Steve tendered his resignation. Within weeks, he formed Berrett-Koehler.

By putting his signature on a vision for how a publishing company should operate, Steve grounded his operation in character and courage. Company stakeholders were to be an eclectic group—vendors, suppliers, authors. Employees would have significant input into strategic decisions. Authors were to be partners, not hired hands. And they were encouraged to deal directly with the entire staff, rather than being assigned to some lone editor who was to act as a buffer.

Authors participated in all aspects of the process, including cover design, book layout, advertising, and marketing. The publisher was to be the caretaker for the authors' work, not its owner. Consequently, authors had the right to pull their book at any time (with thirty days notice) if they were not happy with the quality of Berrett-Koehler's caretaking. Contracts were crafted toward mutual gain, not tilted to favor the publisher. It was a partnership, not servitude.

The publishing industry was aghast. Berrett-Koehler would either disappear in less than a year in the dog-eat-dog world of publishing or become a tiny, quirky boutique that would be more like a vanity press than a force in the industry. After more than ten years of numerous best-sellers, strong profits, and a constant flood of proposals from authors eager to join the BK family, Steve has proven that you can live your values and thrive.

Berrett-Koehler is a company with a conscience. Its ethics are not framed on the wall; they are lived in the hall. The legacy of character is evidenced by the choice of many authors to have BK publish their second and third books. The company was founded on Steve Piersanti's courage to follow his vision. It is maintained by that same courage.

Wear Your Soul on Your Sleeve

The dress-up cocktail party preceded a lavish dinner in historic San Antonio, Texas. The large convention hall was abuzz with excitement and anticipation as more than a thousand sales people enthusiastically shared tall tales and nostalgic memories over grown-up beverages and forceful banners.

It was the annual Eagle Night at GE Betz, a world leader in the engineered chemical treatment of water and process systems in industrial, commercial, and institutional facilities, headquartered in Trevose, Pennsylvania. The special ceremony in San Antonio that night had been choreographed to spotlight a handful of company heroes: those salespeople who were secretly selected both for their superior results and extraordinary talents. Three-time Eagle winners were given not only the bronze eagle statue but also a dress jacket with a gold eagle embroidered on the pocket. While not quite a Master's Green, the jackets were as coveted as the famed golf prize.

Charlie Whitlock, national sales manager and master of ceremonies, outlined the history and significance of the Eagle award as colorful photographs of eagles in the wild adorned the giant screen. He spoke of against-all-odds achievements, an attack-all-barriers attitude, and shining-from-the-core character. Whitlock invited each district manager to share the stage to catalog the accomplishments of the winner from his or her region. When each winning name was called, everyone in the giant hall leapt to their feet to affirm the chosen one. The stunned winners made their way to the lectern while grappling for the proper words to make a fitting acceptance speech. The evening had all the pageantry of the Academy Awards with absolutely none of the ego.

The winners' speeches had much in common. Instead of bravado, there was gratitude; instead of affirmation of self, there was appreciation for team. But most striking were the countless examples of doing what was right for the customer, not always what was profitable. Everyone spoke of taking the high road even though it sometimes meant venturing into challenging, unfamiliar territory and making risky choices. These Eagles were people of principle and exceedingly proud of their tradition, their nobility of purpose, and their dedication to what was best for their customers. Now they were wearing their character not on their sleeves but on their pockets for all to see. W. A. Clarke's clever adage, "You can tell a company by the people it keeps," was never more apropos.

Soul is about substance; sharing soul is about authenticity. And anytime you reveal your authentic substance it is an act of courage, one that invites customers back for a second helping.

Always Be a Solid Citizen

"He's a solid citizen" is an antique expression used to refer to an individual who is both considerate and courageous. It was the label given to a person who was noticeably concerned about the community and others' welfare while also being willing to take an unpopular stand if he or she thought it was the right thing to do. If a "solid citizen" role happened to be in a movie, it almost assuredly went to Jimmy Stewart or Jack Lemmon. If it appeared in a western, it usually landed in John Wayne's saddle.

Service providers who are "solid citizens" win the admiration and loyalty of customers by demonstrating a commitment to their community (in the broadest sense of the word). They are a mix of generosity and courage. They instill trust, foster admiration, and encourage like-mindedness among customers. Solid citizens beget solid citizens.

The Blue Marlin Supermarket on South Padre Island, Texas, looks as though it is still stuck in the fifties. Yet, the large crowd of customers at any time attests to its continued popularity with the locals. The all-purpose grocery store very effectively competes with nearby giants like H-E-B and Wal-Mart. One noticeable difference is the large number of products at the Blue Marlin that have obviously low demand.

"If you did a cost-benefit analysis on some of the items on our shelves, you'd see that the demand is way too low to make these items profitable," says owner Gary Meschi. "You're not likely to find these low-demand products at a Wal-Mart. But we have people who come into our store *because* we carry some of these rarely purchased items. Obviously, you can't take that route on all of your products. We take the approach we do because we see our role as serving our neighbors, not just making a bundle of money."

• • •

The Tattered Cover in Denver continues to enjoy its reputation as the largest independent bookstore in the United States. The bookstore came under attack when owner Joyce Meskis refused to release information about customers as a part of a criminal investigation. Losing in the lower court, she funded an expensive appeal on the grounds that her customers had a right to privacy. Not only did she win the case, she won the admiration of customers around the globe. Even those who disagreed with her stand praised her courage to honor her convictions, even at the risk of significant financial loss.

The secret described in this chapter begins with a word crucial to magnetic service—"reveal." Woven throughout all seven secrets is the spirit of openness, honesty, and legitimacy that such a word implies. Service relationships are given light when there are no barriers to the spirit, soul, and purpose of the organization. When customers say, "I want to see what I'm getting," they are pleading for more than just a visual verification. They want the "real deal"—one that warrants their faithfulness as well as their funds.

Customers today seek a way to put a microscope on what the organization is made of and what it stands for. Only by seeing "inside" can they proceed with the kind of confidence that fuels long-lasting devotion.

• • •

"We need to learn to set our course by the stars, not by the lights of every passing ship."—Omar Bradley

Reflection

Assessing Your Magnetic Service Style

Here is a quick way to assess your "magnetic service" style. This is not a "guess the right answer" inventory, although it should be immediately obvious that the more desirable answers are on the right-hand side of the scale. Simply be honest in your answers. A candid self-assessment now can point to ways in which you can turn yourself and your organization into more magnetic service providers. If you are really brave, ask a few colleagues to provide their assessment of your style using this inventory.

1. Tendency to trust others	Suspicious	1	2	3	4	5	Quick to trust
2. Ease in including others	More of a loner	1	2	3	4	5	More a joiner
3. Comfort with candid feedback	Shun it	1	2	3	4	5	Seek it
4. Degree of risk-taking behavior	Very cautious	1	2	3	4	5	More a maverick
5. Level of openness with others	Reveal little	1	2	3	4	5	Reveal a lot
6. Attentiveness when communicating	Preoccupied	1	2	3	4	5	Very focused

7. Sensitivity to others' feelings	Insensitive	1 2 3 4 5	Sensitive
8. Tolerance of others' differences	Low tolerance	1 2 3 4 5	High tolerance
9. Feelings about your work role	Bored	1 2 3 4 5	Excited
10. Capacity to convey excitement	Hold it in	1 2 3 4 5	Let it out
11. Level of self-understanding	Low	1 2 3 4 5	High
12. Comfort with conflicting views	Low	1 2 3 4 5	High
13. Comfort with change	Uncomfortable	1 2 3 4 5	Comfortable
14. Willingness to value others' views	Rigid	1 2 3 4 5	Open
15. Enthusiasm about learning	Reluctant	1 2 3 4 5	Eager
16. Ease in appreciating humor	Very low	1 2 3 4 5	Very high
17. Degree of versatility	Not versatile	1 2 3 4 5	Very versatile
18. Generosity in relationships	A taker	1 2 3 4 5	A giver
19. Capacity for creative solutions	Resort to policy	1 2 3 4 5	Rely on instinct
20. Motivation for making a big impression	Want to impress	1 2 3 4 5	Want to influence
21. Readiness for partnership	Reluctant	1 2 3 4 5	Ready
22. Ease in cooperating with others	Prefer tension	1 2 3 4 5	Prefer harmony
23. Steadiness in relationships	Unpredictable	1 2 3 4 5	Fairly consistent
24. Reliance on bureaucracy	Focus on rules	1 2 3 4 5	Focus on results
25. Level of integrity	A bit shady	1 2 3 4 5	High integrity
26. Reaction to intense situations	Emotional	1 2 3 4 5	Calm/confident
27. Allegiance to personal values	Lip service only	1 2 3 4 5	Rather courageous
28. Concern for larger community	Self-centered	1 2 3 4 5	Other-centered

Reflection

From *Magnetic Service*, © 2003 by Chip R. Bell and Bilijack R. Bell.

Now, go back and note where your answers were mostly to the left of "3." The table below shows which items correspond to which chapters in the book. As you read the next seven chapters, pay particular attention to the chapter(s) corresponding to these "needs improvement" scores. The chapters to come may offer you special guidance and helpful instruction, as will reviewing the particular corresponding chapter in the first part of the book.

Items 1, 2, 3, 4	Chapter 8 (and Chapter 1)
Items 5, 6, 7, 8	Chapter 9 (and Chapter 2)
Items 9, 10, 11, 12	Chapter 10 (and Chapter 3)
Items 13, 14, 15, 16	Chapter 11 (and Chapter 4)
Items 17, 18, 19, 20	Chapter 12 (and Chapter 5)
Items 21, 22, 23, 24	Chapter 13 (and Chapter 6)
Items 25, 26, 27, 28	Chapter 14 (and Chapter 7)

Reflection

Part Two

The Leadership Side of Magnetic Service

· · · · ·

Magnetic service can occur without leadership. There are people in all sorts of organizations who work to give magnetic service simply out of the belief that customers deserve their best. However, for magnetic service to happen consistently across an organization, leadership has to step in.

The behavior and practices of leaders determine whether magnetic service will be easy or difficult, held in esteem or dismissed as a frill, supported or ignored. Leaders of magnetic service need not be charismatic and charming to be effective. However, they must be clear and sincere about the importance of delivering magnetic service all day, every day. They must be persistent and disciplined in supporting it.

Each of the seven secrets of magnetic service suggests particular roles for the leader to play. This part of the book outlines some of the leadership practices that influence and shape magnetic service. Some are more closely associated with a particular secret. Others really apply across the board. The point is that, taken together, they form a broad picture of the kinds of things a leader can do to promote and support magnetic service.

Fostering Trust

Trust is a verb to customers. It is also a verb to employees. As a verb, it implies aliveness and animation. It constantly needs to be reaffirmed. The leader who fosters trust is the one who never forgets that the word embedded in the middle of "trust" is the word "us."

Trustful leaders care for their employees with the same sense of humanity and consideration that they give their family. In recent years, there has been a shift away from the "family-like" feeling, that was common to agrarian ventures of antiquity. There has also been a shift away from nurturing trust in the workplace. "Family-like" does not connote entitlement, paternalism, or "management by affiliation." It does connote a strong attention to fairness, justice, and compassionate conduct.

When employees experience trust from within the organization, they are quick to demonstrate trust to customers.

Revealing Hopes

If magnetic service is to happen in which customers' hopes, not just needs, are met, leaders must demonstrate that they understand the link between employee relations and customer relations. Magnetic service leaders know that when they listen intently to employees' hopes, employees will listen intently to customers' hopes. They are like Todd Murray, owner of Bäckerei, a Los Angeles bakery that produces artisan breads and rolls for local restaurants and retailers, in appreciating the importance of "dramatic listening." "Even when you have a lot of business," says Murray, "you have to pay attention to customers' needs, hear their complaints, and brainstorm when they want new products. It starts with having a 'customer' perspective with your employees."

Adding Charisma

Charismatic service comes about through the influence of service leaders who are passionate about customers. These leaders attract and retain employees who mirror their daring, boldness, and passion. They see their role as one of being encouraging and affirming, and of nurturing passion. "To succeed," says Scott Cook, CEO of Intuit, "you need people who have a whole bunch of passion, and you can't just order someone to be passionate about a business direction."

Passion comes from having a deep sense of purpose. It is not the result of an "ought to" sense of duty or obligation. Passion is a kind of "can't wait to" enthusiasm. As Milacron's Alan Shaffer said at one of his corporate retreats, "Our goal is not merely to get buy-in. I want to put a lump in their throats and a tear in their eyes. I want to take their breath away."

Being Constant Learners

Magnetic service leaders need to be reflective learners. They must not only know how to learn more about magnetic service from each customer encounter, but also take to heart what Harvard professor and author Rosabeth Moss Kanter has observed: "Leaders are more powerful role models when they learn than when they teach."

Magnetic service leaders know that learning is a never-ending story. They are much like David Smith, CEO of men's wear retailer Pockets, Inc., who compares his fashion leadership role to that of Sisyphus, the mythical character who was cursed with having to roll a big stone to the top of a hill only to have it roll to the bottom again. "We have to recreate ourselves every season," he says. "Every season is like a giant stone we roll in an uphill economy. However, we get the opportunity to walk back down the hill at the end of the season as we reflect on what we have learned that will help us with the next big push up that hill. We use quality time to do quality thinking about quality service improvement."

Making Miracles

Giving the customer an occasional miracle requires creating an atmosphere of innovation. Magnetic service leaders are innovators. They seek out people who are doing new and different things in order to provide them support, eliminate obstacles, and ensure that their different drum beat always keeps them marching. They take the heat for these mavericks. They do not view their job as that of babysitter to employees. "People who want their boss to be a babysitter," says Aurora Health Care CEO Ed Howe, "are the exact same employees who have twelve reasons for why something cannot be done."

Magnetic service leaders are tolerant of eccentricities, choosing to pay more attention to results than style, opting to see special gifts in their organization's innovators instead of odd ways. They know that substance is more crucial than approval and affability.

Promoting Comfort

Super comfortable service happens in a work world that operates like a well-oiled machine. It happens in settings in which partnership is valued and inter-unit competition is shunned. Magnetic service leaders also know that super comfortable service is the by-product of big, compelling goals and a deep belief in their associates' capacity to achieve them. Thriving on pushing-the-limits aims, employees respond to leaders who share their intoxication for challenge. Affirmed by a leader's belief in them, they dig even deeper into the foundation of determination, producing award-winning, story-making, record-breaking performance that ensures customer devotion.

Baring Soul

Magnetic service has character—the kind that promotes "clean" dealings and results in customer trust. The magnetic service organization is an ethical enterprise, one that has a courageous leader at the helm. The nature of organizations, with their propensity for conformity and their aversion to dissonance and disorder, makes bravery something that can be arduous to marshal. But magnetic service leaders invariably manage to bring spunk and soul to the table. Are they always confident and self-assured? Of course not! Sometimes, they take the courageous path with their stomach in their throats, but they take it, nonetheless.

• • •

We use the label "leader" to frame the second part of this book. We define leaders as those people who influence others to achieve important goals. Leadership often has little to do with being a manager, supervisor, or boss. Managers can be good leaders. But leadership can also come from the security guard who alerts the plant manager that a seemingly happy customer had disparaging words to say as he left the facility. It can come from the gate attendant who directs snacks be taken from the grounded plane to the waiting area to serve weary passengers who are unable to board due to a weather delay. Or it might come from a battle-worn nurse who privately but sternly asserts her concern for a patient's welfare to a "too busy to listen" physician.

Effective leaders guide, inspire, support, and encourage. Leaders are the keepers of the organizational values and the perpetuators of standards of excellence. Leaders don't make magnetic service happen alone. But they clearly play a vital role in establishing it through an organization and ensuring that it stays.

Chapter 8

Trust Thrives When Leaders Lead Naturally

**magnetism \ 'mag-nə-,ti-zəm ** *n* : A magnet will reliably perform as it always has—its draw is one of the absolute laws of nature.

**magnetic service \ mag-'nə-tik 'sər-vəs ** *n* : Magnetic service is trustworthy. It continually updates and reaffirms the customer's perception of reliability in the service provider.

Time for a short pop quiz! Take all your books off the desk (except for this one) and take out a pencil. You can put your name at the top of this page if that helps you get in your best "test-taking" mode! In the six scenarios below, select the answer that is most like what you would do. If you do not have an immediate family, assume for the questions that you do. Ready? Begin.

1. *You want very much for your immediate family members to be open and honest in their dealings with you. You are eager to have relationships that lack suspicion or mistrust. Would you:*

A. Periodically sit down as a family and talk through thorny issues and conflicts, openly resolving all you can on the spot, or:

B. Hire a colleague to prepare an anonymous, written attitude survey he would administer to your family members and then come to dinner one evening to present the results, still protecting each family member's anonymity.

2. *Using a participative style, you frequently have encouraged your immediate family members to help you identify ways to make home management more efficient and effective. Without warning, your spouse is unemployed and you must make major cuts in your family budget. Do you:*

A. Ask family members to help you solve the challenges of the economic crunch just like you have sought their input in better times, or

B. Encourage your oldest child to join the army early and send two of the kids off to live with a distant cousin several states away.

3. *You are working in the yard with your oldest child, who is mowing the lawn wearing earphones tuned to the ballgame. Absentmindedly, your eldest accidentally drifts over to the neighbor's yard, mowing down the neighbor's newly planted rose bush. Do you:*

A. Require your child to go immediately to the neighbor, explain exactly what happened, and insist on replacing the rose bush from allowance money, or

B. Wait until your neighbor discovers the missing rose bush and then blame the incident on the fact that the neighbor failed to put an obvious stake beside the new bush that would have prevented your child from mowing it down.

4. Your youngest child answers the phone just as you are about to sit down to dinner. She tells you it is your boss who is apologizing for calling you at home but has a quick, important question. Do you:

A. Take the call, thanking your boss for calling you at home, or

B. Tell your child to tell your boss you're not taking any calls after 6 p.m. and to call back in the morning after 8 a.m.

5. Your best friend stops by your house late one afternoon after having an emotional and difficult conflict with the bank. Practically in tears, the neighbor has come to seek your advice. Do you:

A. Listen intently to your best friend's rendition of the entire incident and then problem solve with your friend to find the best approach, or

B. Immediately inform your neighbor of the bank's solid reputation and suggest your neighbor go back to the bank and apologize for the conflict.

6. Your family has gone high tech over the last few years. Currently, each family member has his or her own computer linked to every other computer in the house. You know quality communications is important to quality family relationships. Do you:

A. Insist the family not give up the open family discussion you have had twice weekly for several years, or

B. Require each family member to check his or her e-mail from family members at least daily and respond to all e-mails within a twenty-four-hour period.

Time's up! Pencil down. The answers to all six of these dilemmas should have been super easy no-brainers. And any of us could add to the list many, many more dilemmas just like these. The answers come easily because our personal relationships are generally authentic and unencumbered by the complex policies, politics, or power plays we encounter in our professional relationships.

The Nature of Leading Naturally

Leaders create an atmosphere of trust when they treat the work environment as the setting for special and important relationships. People who lead from this perspective bring completely different practices than those who have a more paternal or top-down view of the leadership role. Their every action shows that they treat their work groups in much the same way they do their close friends and family. It all adds up to what we call leading naturally. Customers lower their shields of distrust when dealing with an organization that exudes trust.

Napolean Barragan, CEO of Dial-A-Mattress, a company that promises two-hour home delivery, makes the point this way: "Those people in the 5 x 5 cubicles won't put themselves on the line with the customer if they don't trust us to back them up, to treat them as fairly as we expect them to treat customers." Fostering trust requires the front line communicating to customers what management resonates to them.

Think back about the pop quiz that opened this chapter. The obviously correct "A" answers captured the naturalness of wholesome relationships—the stuff trust is made of. Translating the "B" answers from the family scenes into a work context would yield such all too familiar practices as:

- Asking for open employee relationships and then conducting an *anonymous* attitude survey,

- Soliciting ideas from employees when times are good, but then laying those same employees off in tough times instead of seeking their input and help,

- Avoiding culpability and obfuscating responsibility when we know we caused a service breakdown,

- Forgetting that the customer is "the boss" when he or she makes a unique request,

- Being quick to advise or blame and slow to listen when employees or customers have a problem,

- Allowing the exchange of data to replace real, interpersonal communication, complete with face-to-face dialogue and understanding.

Magnetic service is trust—full service practiced in a natural way. It comes from leaders who seek a purer path rather than an artificial approach. Such leaders rely on methods of interaction that they employ in their most valued relationships rather than those that are based on artificial structures and contrived pecking orders. In the agrarian days, work relationships involved the extended family. The family in the field was the family at home. As industrialization created "work for hire" and efficiency-driven "objectivity," people became more like objects and less like relations. While work has clearly become more humanistic over the years, the residues of managerial detachment and indifference still linger.

It takes trustful leadership to consistently yield trustful service. It requires an attitude and an approach that communicates that "associates are like family." In a magnetic service culture, people are encouraged to be creative rather than expected to be compliant. The front line is rewarded for unique practices instead of instructed to follow uniform procedures. Magnetic service is provocative without provoking; unique without being unstable. Customers experience it as having a wholesome, fresh quality. It is thus something that customers trust.

As customers, we are too often confronted with front-line dialogue that is canned, contrived, and contained, or front-line action that is insensitive, preoccupied, or lifeless. If service fails, the service provider tries to turn it into our fault. Such an attitude leads to a marketplace with too many attorneys and too little authenticity. It is a marketplace that is driven by unnatural leadership practices. When leaders take the "us" out of employee trust, they create an atmosphere in which the front-line focus is not on delivering magnetic service but on self-interest, safeguards, and suspicion.

Leading naturally is about behaving at work in much the same way one should behave at home. As one senior exec put it, "When I think about how I should lead, I try to pretend my ten-year-old son and eight-year-old-daughter are members of my staff. Not in the sense that I should be parent-like, but in the sense that I should always be fair, honest, considerate, and a really good role model."

Trust Is Fostered by Optimistic Leaders

Parents who seek to have their children proceed into the world with confidence and trust typically communicate optimism. "Look on the brighter side," "It's not as bad as you think," or "It will all be better in the morning," are the kinds of phrases they rely on to soothe a child's anxiety. They also create in the child calm, confidence, and trust.

Magnetic leaders who seek to create an atmosphere of trust are optimistic about their world and their associates. Optimism does not need to be Pollyanna-ish. It is based, instead, on courageous hope and rock solid conviction in one's capacity to negotiate troubled waters. Optimistic leaders are not fearless, they are just gutsy.

Leaders who foster trust in relationships have a clear idea of what the relationship ought to be like. They also are clear in communicating that expectation. They enter relationships with optimism, hope, and conviction that all will go well. Magnetic service leaders also ground their optimism in a belief that cracks in any relationship can be filled and repaired through honest and respectful communication. Best does not mean perfect; great relationships are never perfect. But good leaders keep striving to make them better.

Trust Requires Honesty

Magnetic service leaders who seek to create a trusting climate work diligently to always assert the truth. This proactive gesture keeps integrity at the forefront of all dealings. "One of the surest signs of a bad or declining relationship is the absence of complaints. Nobody is ever THAT satisfied, especially not over an extended period of time. The person is either not being candid or not being contacted." These words of Harvard professor and marketing guru Ted Levitt were written about customers in his classic *Harvard Business Review* article, "After the Sale is Over . . . " They could just as easily be describing *all* relationships. The absence of unabashed candor reflects the decline of trust and the deterioration of the relationship.

Ask anybody what he or she believes to be the number one cause of divorce. After a few cute answers—like "marriage"—eight in ten will tell you "communication." A key part of maintaining special and important relationships is straight talk, the two-way pursuit of truth. No relationship is likely to be perfect all the time. The healthy work relationship, like the healthy marriage, is marked by candor and welcomed critique. Honesty fuels more honesty if defensiveness is put on the shelf. And as candor triggers improvement, the relationship emerges with greater health.

Trust Occurs When Leaders Respect Others

Respect is a combination of admiration and honoring. When we respect someone, we admire who they are and/or what they do. We experience either an "I wish I could . . . like they can" type of awe or an "I know how hard it is to . . . like they do" type of appreciation. Honoring a relationship means ascribing value to it. Magnetic service leaders do this by seeking ways to bring accolades and praise to their relationships with customers and employees.

Respecting employees is also about giving them elbowroom—to be unique, to be different, and to be special. Relationships marked by possessiveness are relationships that cease to grow. Employees in overprotected relationships may initially feel secure and therefore valued. However, in time they will come to view someone's possessiveness over them as a form of suspicion or mistrust. An initial feeling of security ultimately will be transformed into one of disdain and of being devalued.

Riverside Health Care in Newport News, Virginia, experienced a major loss in 2002. Education Manager Jean Raines unexpectedly passed away. This loss was particularly challenging. It was not that people thought Jean would be there forever. She had already worked more than forty years for Riverside. It was the fact that Jean honored the people who worked around her.

Jean Raines did more than pass out accolades. She visibly demonstrated her devotion to her associates. She nurtured, celebrated, remembered, teased, affirmed, and supported. As a part of her eulogy at her standing-room-only funeral, Riverside EVP Caroline Martin said this about Jean: "She honored *all* of us by the way she showed her abiding love for *each* of us." Adequate leaders show a love for their work. Good leaders show a love for their organization. Magnetic service leaders show "an abiding love for each of us."

Trust Arises When Promises Are Kept

Reliability forms the foundation of trust; trust serves as the glue of magnetic service relationships. Keeping promises is about protecting the sacredness of commitments. It is about caring enough to remember. "Relationships live or die by promises kept," says Marcia Corbett of CLG, Inc. "Reliability is being able to meet every promise, every time," advises Carlo Medici, president and general manager of Bracco Diagnostics in Princeton, New Jersey.

"Keeping agreements," say Gay Hendricks and Kate Ludeman in their book *The Corporate Mystic,* is "joining forces with the creative powers of the universe, the same power that makes oak trees where no trees were before. Having stepped into unity with the creative force in the universe, you need to make good on the creation or cancel it out cleanly. Otherwise, you are bucking the greatest power there is."

"You are only as good as your word" was advice you may have heard growing up. "A person's word is his bond," you may have read. All of these old maxims are borne out by Texas A&M professor Len Berry's service quality research, which affirms that the number-one attribute of service quality from the customer's perspective is reliability. The research on leaders' relationships with associates reveals similar findings. Promises kept lend relationships security in the way that courage lends them adventure.

• • •

We commonly use the word "natural" to refer to things that are pure or organic, meaning that no bad stuff has been added. We also use it to mean innate or native, as in referring to one's natural talent. Magnetic service requires leadership that reflects a purity of purpose as well as good instincts. This does not mean that leadership cannot be learned or refined. It simply means that magnetic service leadership draws on the genetic material of human relationships that are as untainted as children at play and as wholesome as a family sharing a special moment.

• • •

"Customers who consider our waitresses uncivil should see the manager."—Sign in a restaurant

Chapter 9

Hopes Spring Forth When Leaders Foster Revelation

magnetism The characteristic force or draw of a magnetic field has a relatively short range, only impacting another object when close up.

magnetic service Magnetic service is intimate. It is grounded in an understanding of the customer's unspoken hopes, dreams, and aspirations, which can only be obtained through a close, direct relationship.

Revelation. It is a word that does double duty. As it relates to magnetic service, it represents both cause and effect.

One aspect of revelation can be seen in its root "to reveal"—meaning "to expose, make known, or indicate by signs or symbols." Self-revelation on the part of a customer is something that offers you a glimpse of the dreams beneath his or her needs and the aspirations underlying his or her expectations. Customers make such revelations only if the front-line service provider demonstrates respect, understanding, empathy, and confidence. These qualities are found in employees who feel good about who they are and what they do, and that "feel good" can be nurtured by leaders who create a setting of safety.

Magnetic service leaders, in turn, create a setting of safety precisely by embracing the concept we are talking about here: revelation. In other words, they open up, exposing themselves to full view. This, in turn, enables front-line employees to better exude to customers the message of "you can be open with me." Bottom line: leader revelation produces employee safety; employee safety begets customer revelation.

Revelation also means "an eye-opener or a surprise." When customers reveal their hopes and aspirations, the service provider's assumptions or conjectures about the customer are erased. Knowing the customer's needs and expectations gives the service provider a target for good customer service. Learning about the customer's hopes and aspirations positions the service provider to deliver magnetic service. The effect? As a customer might say, "Fulfill my requirements and I will return to you; fulfill my dreams and I will be devoted to you."

The leader's role in customer revelation has to do with what they do to and for employees. The safe haven they create bolsters employees' self-esteem, enhances confidence, and encourages curiosity—all of which are important qualities that front-line service people must have in order to find out what's motivating customers at the deepest level. Leaders create safety through honesty and authenticity, and by expressing acceptance of and appreciation for others.

Revelation-Driven Leaders Employ Dramatic Listening

"But you don't listen to me." A teenage boy shot the age-old line point-blank at his frustrated father in the heat of their verbal battle. The words ricocheted across several neighborhood yards. And it lassoed everyone in earshot into involuntary eavesdropping.

"What do you mean?" his father defensively. "I listen to you all the time." The father and son were engulfed in an awkward silence after the next heart splitting line.

"You and mom listen to me *talk*," said the boy, "but my friends listen to what I *say*!"

Organizations around the country brag about their commitment to great customer listening. Some show off their industrial-strength survey research and their heavy-duty statistics. Others boast about how often their executives talk with customers or sit behind a one-way glass at a focus group. With all the listening, one wonders if anyone is actually hearing anything that's being said.

The teenager mentioned earlier was looking to be valued, not just heard. Today's customers and employees similarly feel over-surveyed and undervalued. Too much effort goes into listening to customers and employees *talk* rather than their meaning. Too often the pursuit is for facts rather than feelings; conversation instead of candor.

Leadership connections are like electrical connections. The greatest power comes from connections that are grounded and on the same wavelength. When interactions between leaders and employees are grounded in honesty and characterized by mutuality and equality, employees become committed to the organization's goals. And, operating from that wavelength, employees become much more focused on customers and on communicating from a straightforward, solid (no BS) position.

Revelation-Driven Leaders Assertively Act on What They Learn

Magnetic service leaders blend attentive listening with rapid action. Alphagraphics is a chain of quick-copy print shops around the country. The store near Southern Methodist University in Dallas is known for their on-the-spot responsiveness to customer input. "What are some ways we act differently from what we say or promise?" asked manager Butch Clarke of a loyal customer one day as the customer was picking up a print job. Butch is famous for his unique ways of querying customers—and loyal customers get the most queries.

"Well," the customer responded, "you talk about delivering the right job right at the right time, but I don't see a clock anywhere. Why don't you put a big school house wall clock where your employees and the customers can see it?"

"Great idea!" Butch responded. He opened the cash register, pulled out a $20 bill and turned to an associate. "Steve, take this money to Eckerd's at the end of the block and buy us a big battery-operated clock to put on the wall right there. We can do the paperwork later."

The move was dramatic, a vivid symbolic gesture for the customer and employees alike. No sooner had Butch heard an improvement idea from a frequent customer, he was swinging into action to implement the idea right in front of the customer. What kind of response do you think he got the next time he asked this customer for a suggestion? What message did Butch convey? No, you can't instantly implement every idea a customer suggests. And customers don't expect that you will. What's most important to them—what really makes them light up—is knowing that they are valued.

Magnetic service leaders have a strong "can do" drive for implementation. Granted, there is great value in careful planning and thoughtful preparation. However, until there is execution, all plans are perfect; no preparation inadequate. Execution spotlights all. It is easy for people to get enamored with the preliminaries since there are no consequences. As Tom Peters and Bob Waterman communicate in their book *In Search of Excellence,* leaders must break the "paralysis from analysis" and push for a "bias for action." Sometimes, it is better to crash moving forward than to crumble standing still.

Revelation-Driven Leaders Sincerely Affirm Others

"Don't ever hire someone you'd be reluctant to hug," a highly successful CEO said to a group of young executives at their leadership training session. His counsel was clearly a departure from the ancient management axiom that says: You don't have to like the people you work with, you just have to respect them.

This particular CEO was not trying to turn the workplace into a country club or fraternity house. Nor was he advocating that leaders be jovial huggers; some people are uncomfortable with public displays of affection. He was rather affirming a belief that great customer service emerges from a culture of affiliation and affirmation. When happy employees communicate self-assurance to customers it fosters an "I trust you" magnetism that draws out customer aspirations. When people work around people they genuinely like and enjoy, their enthusiasm spills over into their dealings with customers.

The CEO was also implying that great leaders never opt to create an obstacle to expressing affection. Watch leaders in organizations that are known for great service. Without exception, they are quick to affirm others, often with a physical gesture. With warm nods, pats on the back, or big bear hugs, magnetic service leaders boldly and obviously express kinship with their associates. Some are, in fact, shy and feel somewhat awkward expressing affection. Yet, they rocket past their own internal reluctance because they so deeply value the positive impact that affirming others has on people. As humorist Thornton Wilder said, "You can buy a pretty good dog, but you can't buy his tail wagging."

Employee confidence is supported through signs of affirmation. Ever thought about the role of cheering at an athletic event? We don't watch games in silence. That's because our intent is to encourage, support, and coax. When sports announcers speak of the "home field advantage," they are acknowledging the power of affirmation as a tool for summoning confidence.

Revelation-Driven Leaders Demonstrate Authenticity and Humility

"This is a no-games zone," the sign read in a cubicle at one of the facilities of OMI, Inc., the 2000 Malcolm Baldrige National Quality Award winner. Headquartered in Englewood, Colorado, the highly respected water treatment company prides itself in being free of politics, gamey behavior, and "stab you in the back" derisiveness. Leaders diligently and sincerely support the people who are supporting the customer. CEO Don Evans sees it this way: "When you ask associates what's different about OMI, the answer is almost always the same: 'Here, people ask me what I think.' Our servant leadership style empowers each associate to amaze the customer."

Discovering the hopes behind customer needs takes place only in an environment that values authenticity and humility. While leaders in such organizations are typically confident, they are as quick to apologize for an error as they are to register modest pride over an achievement. Being humble does not require that you fall on your sword. Nor does it mean that you loudly advertise your warts and clay feet. But it does mean that you work very hard to be open and vulnerable with associates. Open means approachable; vulnerable means unguarded. Such qualities require deliberately stripping any nuances of rank, power, or status from relationships.

• • •

When customers are in the presence of service providers who exhibit respect, understanding, empathy, and self-assurance, they are more confident in sharing their hopes, more honest in articulating their candor, and more enthusiastic in helping the service provider "get it right" in fulfilling their desires.

Magnetic service leaders know how important revelation is in fostering respect, understanding, empathy, and self-assurance among employees. They have learned how to open themselves up to others and how to encourage others to do the same. They know how to use the power of dramatic listening, assertive action, and sincere affirmation in genuine, honest relationships with everyone they deal with. They understand how, in time, all this leads to closer, more direct connections with customers.

• • •

"There is a difference between getting what you pay for and what you hope for."—Malcolm Forbes

Chapter 10

Service Can Be Charismatic If Leaders Exhibit Boldness

magnetism A magnetic force only interacts with physical materials that can conduct electricity.

magnetic service Magnetic service is electrifying. It interacts with customers in a way that conveys excitement, releases passion, and invites customer energy into the relationship.

There is an old expression that goes: "Only dead fish swim with the current." The truth is, smart fish swim in all directions, but the pull of the current does not influence their choice. Magnetic service is, by definition, different from business as usual. Charisma is one of the attributes that separates magnetic service from ordinary good service. Yet we do not mean to say that magnetic service leaders must be charismatic. Leaders who lead only with charisma can be problematic. Charismatic leaders can often be egocentric, drawing attention to their own narcissistic ends rather than inviting collaboration and inclusion.

"Charisma" refers to a spiritual gift or talent or to the personal magnetism associated with some celebrities and political leaders. It connotes a trait, something ingrained, not something that service providers can *do*. Service with charisma, on the other hand, has to do with a willingness to take bold action. It also has to do with trusting your employees enough to encourage boldness.

"Whatever you can do, or dream you can, begin in boldness," wrote German poet-philosopher Johann von Goethe. "Boldness has genius, power, and magic in it." Scottish explorer W.H. Murray echoed the same sentiment when he wrote, "Until one is committed, there is hesitancy, the chance to draw back, always ineffectiveness. . . [T]he moment one definitely commits oneself, then Providence moves, too. All sorts of things occur to help one that would never otherwise have occurred."

Charismatic service is countercultural, unexpected, and goes against the grain. It is sometimes cut of unfamiliar cloth. And while any specific act of charismatic service might not be that unconventional, it springs from a place that is. It is that place—that restless, unsettled place—that leaders must occupy if they are to model and encourage boldness. This is the habitat of ground-breaking pioneers and norm-breaking entrepreneurs. It is also where inventors and artists of all types reside.

Encouraging boldness is more about removing obstacles and impediments than it is about adding in anything different and new. Some biologists would assert that gutsiness is in our genes, but that it has been domesticated by social stigmas and psychological doubts. We were at one time animals in the wild, depending on our cunning and daring for survival. There is no security in nature. Helen Keller observed: "Avoiding danger is no safer in the long run than outright exposure. Life is either a daring adventure or nothing." The "remove rather than add" approach means leaders focus on eliminating whatever exists in the work world that fuels the opposite of boldness—timidity, hesitance, reserve, and the like.

Boldness Is Born of a Higher Purpose

Stoking the flames of boldness starts with a wide-eyed focus on a dream, rather than a squinty-eyed look at the task. Caution and hesitance can come from being mired in day-to-day minutiae. As one loses touch with the "forest vista" because there are too many trees to view, one soon also becomes blind to personal hopes and dreams. "I came to my last job," said one retired senior leader, "with a great sense of purpose. But I got so enmeshed in what I had to do that I soon forgot what I had hoped to be. It was not until I was about ready to retire that I realized I had gotten more defensive and less daring."

Boldness is a choice based on a commitment to a future state. It is not a reaction; it is deliberate action. Revenge, rebellion, and rage are reactionary. Their vigilante quality gives them a caustic edge that is more conducive to destruction than creation. Boldness is pro-action at its finest, a step toward the light. It is born of a noble reach beyond the mediocre of the moment and the ordinariness of the status quo.

Daring without recklessness requires awareness of a vision and a desire to move in the direction of that vision. In the words of motivational writer and speaker Zig Ziglar, "Without a dream there will be no 'dream come true.'" Magnetic service leaders have a valued dream that serves as the compass for their courage and an inspiration to associates who boldly seek to create charismatic service for customers.

"Before you can inspire with emotion," said Winston Churchill, "you must be swamped with it yourself. Before you can move their tears, your own must flow. To convince them, you must yourself believe." Before you can stir ardor for a vision, you must first clear up your own. Review the questions below as you think of where you presently are.

* Why am I here, now, in this role?

* If I were writing my own epitaph and I had to capture the essence of what I achieved while on this earth, what would I want the tombstone to read?

* (Assume you have a six-year old child). When my six-year-old child asks me WHY I did what I did in my professional life, what would I say? ("To make a living" is not an acceptable answer).

* When I feel very fulfilled in my work, what is typically occurring?

* If I learned I had only six months to live, and I HAD to continue to work during that period, HOW would I work? What would I do differently?

What legacy would I want to leave to my industry or profession? My organization? My team or unit?

* If a stranger suddenly died and willed me $10 million after taxes with the stipulation that I had to work in a professional role five days a week, forty-eight weeks a year, how would my work life change? What do the changes indicate about what is really important to me?

After an honest and thoughtful consideration of these questions, consider a few more: What is interfering with your capacity to be daring at work? What actions can you take to eliminate or minimize the barriers to your boldness? What can you do to communicate the vision to your associates? Where do you spend time? What do you show excitement or worry about? Remember: Employees don't watch your mouth, they watch your moves.

Magnetic leaders who are intent on fostering boldness talk often about mission. They focus on what they want the team, unit, or organization to BE, not just what they want it to DO. They communicate the "whys" when making assignments, not just the "whats" and "whens." They recognize heroes by "telling their stories"—especially the details of those accomplishments that demonstrate vision and mission. And, most important, magnetic leaders make sure their actions are consistent with their mission or purpose.

Boldness Happens When Employees Do Not Fear Error

Boldness would not be daring were the potential for error not large. How one deals with error can say volumes about one's commitment to being a magnetic service leader. When leaders meet error with rebuke, they send a very different message than when they see error as an opportunity for learning and problem solving. Are error-making employees quickly labeled as stupid, evil, or lazy? But consider: Isn't it highly unlikely that the person in charge of hiring employees said, "Let me see how many dumb, malicious, or shiftless employees I can hire this week?"

Without risk, there's no creativity. But with risk comes the occasional honest mistake. It's easier to gently rein in an over-zealous, go-the-extra-mile employee than to find one with an enthusiastic attitude in the first place. Fostering boldness is a manifestation of trust. The greater the trust, the greater the freedom. But freedom comes with responsibility. The leader's job is to coach employees to feel more and more comfortable with more and more responsibility.

Examine procedures. Employees may feel vulnerable due to past practices. Are employees clear on what is a "thou shalt not . . . " law versus what is an "it would be better if you didn't . . . " guideline? Are rules of thumb and rules of law treated in the same way? Are metrics so abusive or pervasive that employees feel as though leaders are "pulling plants out of the dirt to determine if they are growing?" Recall a time an employee made an honest mistake. Was forgiveness expressed or just implied? Are employees publicly given the benefit of the doubt? Do they get more coaching or more critiquing? How many times are employees praised for excellent efforts that failed to work? Are employees commended for seeking assistance from others, including other managers?

Boldness Comes from Responsible Risk Taking

Employees need guidelines, not unlimited license. The manager who says, "Just go do whatever you think is best," is probably demonstrating abdication, not encouraging boldness. There have to be some guidelines, but also enough elbowroom for the employee to adapt to the situation and customer. Customers don't want uniformity in service. While they want consistency, they also want to be treated as the unique human beings they are. This requires front-line flexibility.

Risk taking is not a blank check to be foolhardy and reckless. Sensible risk taking comes from knowing how to balance service with stewardship—how to create a unique experience for the customer that is also congruent with the organization. It involves "owner thinking." If employees are to make front-line decisions like owners, they need the benefit of "owner-type information." If employees are to focus on long-term relationships with customers (and not be completely preoccupied with the transaction cost of each encounter) they need big-picture direction and details about the balance sheet.

"A lot of us think that success is about the boldness of the gamble," says Nancy Koehn, professor of business history at Harvard Business School. "Success is more complex. It's about understanding what's bold about the boldness, about knowing how to keep the risk from coming back to bite you, and about knowing what your organization will get from taking such a big step."

Boldness does not imply the absence of fear. People who are daredevils think they are invincible. Their arrogance causes them to miss seeing the signals and cues that are needed as guidance to success. Sometimes hotshots get lucky; in time, they crash and burn. Magnetic service leaders help associates respect fear and channel it. They provide outlets for employees to talk about their apprehensions, and they deliver support and encouragement when employees have doubts.

How do you cultivate responsible risk taking? Examine your reward and recognition practices. Which is more valued: creativity or compliance? Being resourceful or always being right? Who gets praised or promoted—and for what? Former 3M CEO Lew Lehr put it well: "If you place too many fences around people they can easily become pastures of sheep. And how many patents are assigned to sheep?"

The old adage "Birds of a feather flock together" also applies here. Surround your unit with bold people. Seek the counsel and camaraderie of others who exhibit daring and courage. Invite known, card-carrying mavericks to your meetings. Read biographies of pioneers who overcame personal limitations to achieve greatness. Visit organizations known for breakthrough thinking (R&D facilities, art studios, etc.). Ask bold leaders you know to share their recipe for concrete confidence. While the approach you use needs to be relevant to your unit, others can offer helpful suggestions.

Boldness Comes Not Just from Learning, But from Unlearning

"The greatest obstacle to discovery is not ignorance," wrote historian Daniel Boorstin, "It is the illusion of knowledge." The path to boldness begins with an "I don't know" first step, following by an "I could be wrong" second step. Knowledge may give us the confidence to move into the realm of the unknown, but curiosity and interest fuel the move.

Magnetic service leaders create an atmosphere of perpetual experimentation that compels employees to innovate. In this context employees learn that to challenge the status quo is the norm. They will view those who hold on to the past (rather than learning from the past and letting go of what no longer fits) as oddities with short tenures. Creating a climate that embraces experimentation and learning takes humble leaders who are willing to model unlearning. When Rich Teerlink was CEO of Milwaukee-based Harley-Davidson, he began meetings with dealers with the words, "Here is something I screwed up on . . . and what I learned from it." Few organizations in the world value perpetual learning (and unlearning) more than Harley-Davidson.

Emphasize growth-producing experimentation by recognizing employees whose performance stands out. Use them as mentors for others. Allow time in meetings for employees to share key learnings and unlearnings. Be a lifelong learner yourself. Your example is one employees will follow. To repeat Rosabeth Moss Kanter's guidance, "Leaders are more powerful role models when they learn than when they teach." And part of that modeling is public acknowledgement of what you "unlearned" as well as what you learned.

Identify a small but achievable personal niche for your own growth experiment. Find a hobby you can almost perfect. Visit ennobling places. Take time to visit a museum or attend a concert that reflects the best. Visit great hotels—even if your stay is limited to having a drink in their lounge. Listen to great music and educational radio. Tutor a child. Raise the plane of your life. Form a support group of others who are reluctant to be daring. Talk about the consequences of mediocrity as well as the rewards of risk taking.

The late Hallmark Cards artist Gordon MacKenzie, in his best-selling book *Orbiting the Giant Hairball*, tells the story about his time volunteering as an artist-in-residence in the Kansas City-area elementary schools. When he entered a first-grade class he would ask, "How many artists do we have here?" and all the children would raise their hands. The same question asked of third graders yielded only about half the number of raised hands. And when MacKenzie asked sixth graders his question, only one or two tentative "closet" artists would raise their hands. What happened to youthful eagerness? The same thing that can happen in organizations that stifle boldness in their employees.

Service with charisma requires employees with the nerve to eagerly raise their hands. Service with charisma takes leaders with a hankering to have an organization of artists ready to give customers an experience that becomes the subject of memory-making stories.

. . .

Spartacus was a real-life slave who led a massive grassroots uprising against the Roman Empire. The movie about his life was a major hit with a cast of silver-screen giants like Kirk Douglas, Tony Curtis, Jean Simmons, Lawrence Olivier, and Peter Ustinov. In the movie, after the severely outnumbered slaves are defeated in a bloody battle by the Roman Army and several of their allies, the Emperor demands the head of the person who started the slave revolt. Surveying the field of defeated survivors, he announces that if someone reveals which one of them is Spartacus, all but Spartacus will be freed. If no one does, all will be crucified. One by one, each of the hundreds of survivors stands and proudly proclaims, "I am Spartacus."

When magnetic service leaders stand up to be counted, they never stand alone. They stand in the midst of other service providers who not only share their vision and passion, purpose, and spirit but also are itching to turn them all into reality—right now, today.

. . .

"The opposite of courage is not cowardice; it is conformity."—Rollo May

Chapter 11

Curiosity Lights Up When Leaders Learn Out Loud

magnetism A type of natural magnet is a rock called magnetite, which was also called lodestone, or "leading stone."

magnetic service Magnetic service is edifying. It gently leads the customer into service encounters that result in customer learning.

Magnetic service leaders filter every customer encounter through two questions: How can I understand my customer better, and How can I make my customer smarter? Magnetic service leaders nurture the spirit of curiosity by being perpetual insight hunters. They are continually and noticeably on the prowl for new wisdom. They look around the corners for opportunity, feel the power of discovery, and keep an ear to the ground for fresh understanding. They learn all the time. And they learn out loud—meaning that they learn in plain view of everyone.

Magnetic service leaders learn for learning's sake—they get an adrenaline rush out of always honing their skills, enhancing their understanding, and deepening their wisdom. They know that the pursuit of the "not known" is worth more than the praise of the "known." Magnetic service leaders lust for the thrill of the hunt. They are restless, hungry souls who are never satisfied with what they know because they appreciate the fact that "antiquated" is right on their heels and "obsolete" is gaining on them quickly.

At the same time, they continually direct their hunt for insight toward the goal of understanding customers better. "Just when you think you know what customers value," says John Campbell, president of Toronto-based Brookfield Ventures, a large commercial property management company, "some incident happens that reminds you that you still have a lot to learn. It means customer listening is never over."

It also means that questioning customers is a never-ending process. Being continuously curious about customers involves a dogged and determined quest that says, in the words of one world-class car sales professional, "I'll keep asking and listening and nosing around until something lights up." Service providers driven by curiosity know that until the customer "lights up," they have not reached the level of understanding that can truly inform anticipatory action and clairvoyant response.

Create a Culture of Curiosity

A culture that values curiosity is one that is inventive and exciting. Walk into the headquarters of USAA in San Antonio, 3M in St. Paul, or Lockheed Martin in Fort Worth and you can feel the heat of originality emanating from the organizational oven. What you later learn is that you are in a place with an everlasting focus on perpetual growth. The popular label for this kind of environment is a "learning organization." A more accurate description is a "discovering organization." "Learning" can imply the act of adding to or increasing what's already there; "discovering" means uncovering or finding. "Learning" can happen through osmosis, a passive process of growing without making much effort. "Discovering" suggests an active search and a deliberate exploration.

A "discovering" organization is all about curiosity and the intentional pursuit of insight. When Arie de Geus of Royal Dutch/Shell wrote, "Your ability to learn faster than your competition is your only sustainable competitive advantage," he was speaking of the power of the hunt for insight, not the glorification of the attainment of competence. What are the factors common to all "discovering organizations"?

The classic book *The Management of Innovation* by Tom Burns and George Stalker examined the commonalities of the most renowned research and development facilities in the country—those that churned out the most patents, Nobel prizes, and breakthroughs. The punch line was clear and consistent. Discovery was predictable when there were leaders who communicated a clear and compelling purpose, provided a safe and supportive work environment, conveyed high but attainable expectations, and delivered target-seeking feedback that inspired as much as it instructed.

A stroll through Universal Studios Hollywood with theme park president Larry Kurzweil says a lot about his priorities. He warmly greets guests, asks if they are having a great time, and picks up trash. Bill Marriott, Chairman of Marriott Corporation, is passionate about the nobility of service to hotel guests. It is not unusual for a guest to be zealously queried about his or her experience by Mr. Marriott in the hotel lobby or elevator. Kurzweil and Marriott both know that what people see leaders do is more important than what they hear leaders say.

Magnetic service leaders demonstrate their passion for customers by constantly asking questions of managers and employees about the customers' experience. They look for every opportunity to learn and communicate to employees, through their actions, that searching for what is unknown is as important and valuable as acting on what is known.

"Through Peabody Service Excellence® our associates are constantly delivering a level of guest service that is a combination of ongoing training and day-to-day interaction with our guests," said Alan Villaverde, vice president/general manager of The Peabody Orlando. "My job is to ensure that our guests' expectations are exceeded. To achieve this, we don't just observe guests' needs, we ask guests what their needs are, and follow through to final delivery. We are all in a constant learning mode which keeps us up-to-date on the changing requirements of our guests."

Tell Stories to Foster Learning

One of the most powerful tools that magnetic service leaders use to teach others is storytelling. Stories are memorable and rich in their capacity to convey meaning. Stories also stir inquisitiveness and inspire front-line employees to become customer mentors. "We strive to provide legendary service," says Bridget Bilinsksi, VP of franchising for Courtyard by Marriott. "And that means we need legends to remember in order to guide us in creating legends in the future."

"If the Bible were a list of rules," says information design guru Richard Wurman, "it would have been out of print centuries ago." Rather, it is a compilation of stories that have become timeless. It is the power of storytelling that creates legends out of organizational heroes, parables out of organizational errors, and folklore out of organizational beliefs. Anecdote invites discovery.

Stories reveal what norms or mores are unique to the organization. When Southwest Airlines employees tell the story of retired CEO Herb Kelleher hiding in the luggage bin to surprise passengers as they entered the plane, they are *really* saying, "We are supposed to have fun." When Marriott managers tell the story of founder J. Willard Marriott noticing customers buying sandwiches at his Hot Shoppe restaurant near the Washington, D.C., airport to eat on the plane and subsequently his starting the first meal-catering service to the airlines, they are *really* saying, "Take care of customers and look for opportunities to serve." When FedEx employees tell the story of a West Coast front-line employee who authorized a private jet to transport a piece of equipment needed to rescue little Jessica McClure trapped in a well in Texas, they are *really* saying, "We are empowered to make decisions on behalf of our customers."

"When we started telling exceptional service stories at the start of management meetings," says CFO Don Nestor of Aurora Health Care, headquartered in Milwaukee, "it helped our corporate vision become part of the culture of the organization."

Just as great teachers have always used stories to foster learning, great leaders use stories to mold a gathering of people into a partnership of colleagues. If stories are told with consistency, conviction, and clarity, they are heard. If stories are followed by aligned actions and obvious accountability, they are believed. If stories are repeated by those who are not the subject of the tale, they are remembered.

Provide a Curiosity-Supporting Environment

She was one of the most focused children in her neighborhood. You were never able to get past her on a walk without encountering a barrage of intriguing questions. She played piano at three; read fluently at five. Wise beyond her years yet innocent in her manner, she was the darling of every adult in her Birmingham neighborhood. Some of her classmates viewed her maturity, perfectionism, and dainty manners as being prissy; others knew they were witnessing the emergence of an intellectual powerhouse who was destined for greatness.

"I had parents who gave me every conceivable opportunity," she would tell a *Vogue* magazine interviewer. "They also believed in achievement." Her innocent but pointed questions were always met by guests with warmth and affirmation, never disdain. She went to grown-up plays and concerts that her friends thought were boring. She started college at fifteen, becoming a distinguished scholar, an award-winning author and professor at Stanford, an accomplished athlete and pianist—and the National Security Advisor to the President of the United States!

When Dr. Condoleezza Rice speaks of her roots, it is always with allegiance to the supportive and encouraging way in which her parents, John and Angelena Rice, nurtured her curiosity and cultivated her zeal for excellence. People with curiosity come from environments in which others are quick to champion and slow to chastise. Their inquiring minds are celebrated not just by ovations but also by opportunities to pursue their curiosity in ever more stimulating ways.

Communicate Clear Expectations

Doug Denton, SVP and chief information officer of credit card giant MBNA, describes the company's focus on employee support this way: "We like to say that it all begins with an attitude: Satisfy the Customer. And it's Customer with a capital 'C,' by the way. This attitude drives everything we do, and it's what separates us from the competition. It's an attitude that drives people to get things done, instead of looking for excuses. It's an attitude that says, 'I'm going to take charge of this Customer's issue and resolve it to his or her satisfaction, no matter what it takes.' Our people know that a life-long Customer is better than a one-time Customer, so they look at the long term and, because they have the right attitude, they instinctively know to do the right thing for the Customer. Everything that happens at MBNA is a direct result of the attitude of the people who work here."

The experience of support (versus the *promise* of support) comes about when leaders spend priority time running interference, providing important resources, and using valuable time to listen and learn about employee needs and requirements. It happens when employees witness leaders assuming the best about their associates and being quick to defend (and slow to critique) when excellent efforts yield mixed or negative results. It is affirmed when error provokes reflection and problem solving rather than an ominous search for a culprit.

Lockheed-Martin depends on super-bright, highly creative engineers to make the necessary breakthroughs in air defense that ensure long-term military preparedness. Despite the "analytical squared" nature of some of their engineers, they manage to win major defense contracts and craft Star Wars-like defense systems. Their victory in the intensely fought battle for the coveted Joint Strike Fighter project, the richest government contract in United States history, came from showing uncommon curiosity about their customer's needs, expectations, hopes, and aspirations.

"After winning the $200 billion project that competitor Boeing had hoped to win," reports senior manager and Lean Sigma program director Mike Joyce, "We did two important things. We found ways to get inside our customers' heads by teaching our people to be relentlessly inquisitive. We staged countless focus groups with contractors and customers to unearth their blunt honesty on 'the good, the bad, and the ugly.' But we also fueled that 'expectation expedition' by conveying high expectations to our people. Some would say we won the JSF contract because we truly believed we would."

Magnetic service leaders are clear about their expectations and enthusiastic about communicating them. Hugh McColl, retired chairman of Bank of America, is credited with taking the company from being the thirtieth largest bank (when it was North Carolina National Bank) to the second largest bank in the United States. While the media enjoyed focusing on his flamboyant and forceful public persona, those who worked directly for him found him to be both a compassionate and determined leader. "He was very direct about his high expectations," said retired EVP Chuck Cooley, "and he was there in the trenches with you, always learning and constantly supporting. I worked with Hugh for thirty years. He enjoyed developing winners as much as he liked to win. No one was ever bored working for him."

Teach Through Target-Seeking Feedback

"Honest criticism," wrote Franklin Jones, "is hard to take, particularly from a relative, a friend, an acquaintance, or a stranger." Yet, feedback is vital for lending direction to human energy. It is also crucial for fostering a discovery-oriented atmosphere.

Ken Blanchard is credited with calling the word "feedback" the "breakfast of champions." Ken was giving us more than a clever sound bite by borrowing from the tag line from the Wheaties® cereal ad. When you dissect the word into its parts—"feed" and "back"—you get the intended connotation of feedback as a tool for nurturing wisdom. Think of it as discovery fuel. And breakfast is the most important meal of the day (we literally "break fast"). So Blanchard's quote is indeed meaningful on a number of levels.

Target-seeking feedback is the kind that not only fuels, it inspires. It focuses on goal-oriented improvements that a person can make rather than on mistakes of the past. It is delivered in the future tense. Coaching guru Marshall Goldsmith calls it "feedforward," meaning that when we engage in it, we offer suggestions for the future (the target) instead of statements about the past. Rather than delivering proof about what already happened, target-seeking feedback attempts to unearth potential. It does not say "You were in error when you . . . ," but asks, "What might be the impact of your . . . ?" Rather than focusing on culpability, target-seeking feedback concentrates on capability. Traditional feedback looks back; target-seeking feedback leans forward.

How do leaders give target-seeking feedback intended to fuel discovery? They start by creating a climate of identification—with comments that have an "I'm like you"—that is, not perfect or flawless—message. They state the rationale for the feedback, ensuring there is a clear way for the recipient to make sense of it. The person is not left wondering, "Why is she telling me this?" or "How in the world can I benefit from that?"

Besides being clear and empathetic, target-seeking feedback is straightforward and honest. This does not mean blunt or cruel; it means that the recipient is not left wondering, "What did she *not* tell me that I needed to hear?" Trust is born of clear communication. Magnetic service leaders ask themselves, "How would I deliver this feedback if I were giving it to myself?" They take their cues from their own preferences, giving feedback as they would want to receive it.

. . .

Magnetic service leaders set a powerful tone when they show that they are willing and able to "learn out loud," in front of others, as well as encourage others in never-ending discovery. Customers are more confident in organizations that visibly learn—and keep learning. Customers are more devoted to organizations that pass the gift of growth to them. Growing customers is not just a marketing concept. It is a customer devotion concept that begins with leaders who are conspicuously zealous about learning.

. . .

"The prime business of business is learning."—Harrison Owen

Chapter 11 : Curiosity Lights Up When Leaders Learn Out Loud

Chapter 12

Miracle Making Happens When Leaders Inspire Engagement

magnetism A magnetic field cannot be seen with the naked eye; however, its pull can be felt and observed through its works.

magnetic service Magnetic service is unexpected. It comes from a deep understanding of what customers value, which service providers learn by invisible means but demonstrate in surprising ways.

The scene was a corporate cliché—the annual management meeting. There was the usual banner, banter, and baked potato. The CEO was about to begin his eighty-slide "state of the company" PowerPoint® presentation. Tom was a consultant to the company and sat as a guest at a table of eight managers toward the back of the hotel ballroom.

The guy beside Tom leaned over and knowingly whispered, "He doesn't give a rat's butt about the managers here tonight." He paused to gauge Tom's response, and then continued: "Our benefits suck, we have to stay in cheap hotels when we're on the road, and he took away the daycare, casual Friday, and office parties at Christmas time." Before Tom could respond, the lights lowered, and the CEO started his show.

The CEO by no means seemed to be the ogre described by Tom's seatmate. He convincingly outlined his rationale for austerity and sacrifice. His slides painted an unmistakable picture of economic challenge. But instead of doom and gloom, the CEO spoke of hope and opportunity. Rather than dwell on the errors of the past, he delivered his enthusiasm for the future.

His passion was indisputable; his words, inspirational. He closed by inviting his top management team to the stage. One by one, he complimented their unique contribution with a sentence or two about each manager's primary mission in the weeks ahead. Tom himself was super psyched by the end of the presentation—ready to rush out and sell something—and he was just a guest!

The lights came up, the audience warmly applauded, and the group on the stage marched off in harmony. Tom looked around to see that most attendees were visibly moved by the stirring call to action. Their nods were up and down rather than side to side. Their buzz had a supportive tone.

But Tom's seatmate was unmoved. "See what I mean," he announced. "Not a single word about what he's going to do for us out here in the trenches!" Though he wanted to say, "There's no crying in baseball!" Tom could see this guy was not interested in letting go of either his position of entitlement or his disappointment in not getting his share. Tom walked away wondering, "What lessons do you think this man's attitude teaches his kids about life and work?"

A good question, to which we would add: And what insights into the leadership side of magnetic service can we glean from Tom's experience? How would a magnetic service leader take the employee's attitude and turn it into grist for greatness instead of grumbling grudges? How would you help others in your organization shift the focus from self-absorption to self-determination, from mediocre to miracle-making?

Help People Feel Whole, Not Just Good

Miracle-making service comes from front-line associates who are givers, not takers. When people lack self-esteem and feel "owed" by life, they typically operate from a scarcity mentality. Those who feel whole—meaning they feel good about who they are and doing what they do—delight in opportunities to enchant others.

Leaders who focus solely on helping people feel good can deliver a superficial, short-term fix that does little to employees' sense of wholeness. Cheerleaders and motivational speakers make us feel good, not strong—or they make us feel better about being weak. The emotional veneer, while pleasant and enjoyable, fails to be the substance that fills the internal reservoir of self-esteem.

What creates wholeness? People feel whole when they are engaged. An idle mind is not only the devil's workshop; it is the garbage dump for doubt, fear, and anxiety. Examine the emotional by-products of unemployment or the transitional challenges some face as they retire. It is the leader's job to create a workplace where people can be fully engaged, where their talents and skills are optimized.

People feel whole when they are engaged in work that has meaning and purpose. When work is required but not valued, the toiler gets the message that he or she is without worth. But when work is connected to a cause, vision, or purpose, the toiler feels validated and valued. In the words of Max DePree, the former CEO of furniture manufacturer Herman Miller, "The first responsibility of a leader is to define reality. The last is to say thank you." Defining reality means communicating the vision and helping people see the connection between their "brick laying" actions and the "cathedral building" aim.

People feel whole when they are challenged and stretched. If the individual capacity is present, the standard is arduous, and the encouragement is reliable, challenges become a magnet that draws the best from people. The result is the kind of personal confirmation that bolsters self-esteem. The leader's role is to model the standard and be relentless in ensuring that all abide by it.

Engaged, purpose-seeking achievers are filled with self-esteem. They feel so filled (some would say blessed) that they are anxious to share their gifts with others. This provides the impetus for the pursuit and perpetuation of miracle-making for the customers they serve.

Carry the Flag, Not the Water

A new principal took over the leadership of an elementary school where the students had mediocre scores on the year-end achievement tests. Her mission was clear: create an environment in which students learned better and more. The new principal's predecessor shared with her little about the staff or the past, but offered strong advice: "Take real good care of my precious teachers." The faculty meeting on the first day of school painted the picture clearly. As most teachers entered the school library for the meeting, their first words were bitter: "Where are our donuts? We ALWAYS get big donuts!"

Leaders are not surrogate parents. Their job is to communicate a clear mission (carry the flag), communicate a passion for that mission, provide tools needed to carry out that mission, and communicate both encouragement and affirmation along the way. Leaders carry neither water—nor big donuts.

Carrying the flag is the leader's preeminent responsibility. It means having a solid sense of where you hope to go—a picture in your head of what it will be like to reach the aim. And it means pursuing that picture unwaveringly.

Stew Leonard's Dairy is one of the country's most famous grocery stores. Located in several cities in Connecticut, it was listed in the *Guinness Book of World Records* as having the highest sales per square foot of any retail establishment in the world. Shortly after Stew, Sr., passed day-to-day leadership to Stew Leonard, Jr., renowned Harvard Business School professor Michael Porter was invited to lead a long-range strategic planning meeting. Since it was Stew, Jr.'s first planning session as the CEO, Stew, Sr., decided not to attend. Just as the meeting was about to begin, Stew, Sr., called to the meeting room to report that a customer had complained that the grapes tasted flat.

"Oh, Dad," exclaimed Stew, Jr., "I am so glad you called! Dr. Porter is here to start our strategic planning meeting. Let me put you on the speakerphone so you can give us all your thoughts on your vision of the company."

There was a long silence on the speakerphone. Then Stew, Sr. repeated a single sentence that said it all: "A customer complained that the grapes tasted flat." No one doubted the focus and priority after that.

Magnetic service leaders know the link between vision and action. They have a profound understanding that—to paraphrase a quote found on the wall of an old church in Italy—vision without action is daydreaming, but action without vision is random activity. Magnetic service leaders spend time conceptualizing the vision, communicating that vision, and acting in ways that both reflect and reinforce that vision. When theme park builders suggested to Walt Disney that he take a more cost-effective route and build the Magic Castle last, he balked. "The Magic Castle is the centerpiece and symbol of what Walt Disney World is all about. It must be built first."

Require Execution, Not Excuses

John Patterson is a former senior executive with a major hotel chain. After the hotel was sold to another company, he opted to start a consulting firm headquartered in Atlanta. Several months into his growing consulting practice, he was invited to attend an executive meeting of a brand new client. Scheduled to run for three hours, John was just twenty minutes into it when the outcome was clear. The group had no intention of making the important decisions on their meeting agenda.

"They were involved in a serious game of 'shake and fake,'" reports John. "'Shake and *bake*' is what execs should be responsible for doing," continues John. "They plan and execute. But members of this team, no doubt with more on their plates than each thought reasonable, had one goal: to sound passionate and committed but to exit the meeting with no decisions made that would result in any more 'to do's.'"

John laments about how sad it was to watch a doomed meeting get "pretended" into three hours. And this was the team's normal practice. John also wondered how many times he had engaged in the same game as an executive. "They called themselves executives (as in 'to execute'), but these folks were really executioners—killing the spirit of the company with their collusion to thwart progress."

Magnetic service leaders get things done. They waste neither their time nor that of others with fake rationalizations and excuses. They enjoy the process of accomplishing. And they enjoy the outcome of achievement. They truly believe that closing is as sweet as commencing.

Magnetic service leaders start gatherings by clarifying their mission, communicate the plan for getting to that mission, and do not leave the room without accountabilities clearly defined and assigned. They also take time at the end of each gathering to discuss ways to make the next meeting more effective. They are impatient with loose ends. They have a low tolerance for the unnecessary expenditure of energy and for employees who are more interested in passing the buck than taking the hit when mistakes are identified.

Create Impatience, Not Restraint

"Desperadoes waiting for a train" by Guy Clarke is a song made famous by the Highwaymen, a singing group made up of country music giants Johnny Cash, Kris Kristofferson, Willie Nelson, and the late Waylon Jennings. It perfectly captures the sense of eagerness that magnetic service leaders help create. Watch such leaders in action and there is always a sense of anticipation surrounding them, as though something special is just around the corner. More important, they fan the flame of impatience and expectancy by their low tolerance for anything that creates temperance, moderation, or restraint.

It is not that these leaders are shoot-from-the-hip, impulsive types. Their decisions are grounded in substance and solid information. It is more a recognition that being in the moment is required for greatness.

They speak about the journey ahead with excitement. They evaluate input filtered through an interest in tomorrow, not an anchor to yesterday. They show more fascination with what they can be than they do anxiety with what they are.

Larry Kurzweil, President of Universal Studios Hollywood, requested that the theme park to turn up the volume on the street music and to make it peppy, walking-somewhere music. His leadership style communicates the same upbeat, animated, idea-a-minute attitude. When people are with him, his infectious forward-pushing energy makes them want to push the go button and make things happen. The result? Universal Studios Hollywood enjoys a repeat-visit rate that is considerably higher than that of Disneyland and other theme parks in the area.

View Mediocrity as a Nasty Enemy, Not a Necessary Evil

Mediocrity is the enemy of magnetic service. Mediocrity can sap the energy from passion and the opportunity from initiative. Leaders who tolerate mediocrity signal that their real standards are much lower than those they generally state. Magnetic service organizations in fact can be populated by winners only—people who have a passion for their work and constantly seek to improve their surroundings. The bell-shaped curve in which there will always be a small percentage of superstars and an equal number who do just enough to get by is not a cultural necessity.

Bob Patton, head of SBC Global Markets Customer Care Group, tells his front-line employees to "stand up and be counted or go somewhere else where sitting down is tolerated. We are about passion here. We cannot make you passionate . . . it's something that comes from within you. We are passionate and excited about what we have ahead of us. We will do our best to create an opportunity and a supportive environment for you to contribute with zeal and enthusiasm. But it is partly up to you. And if you can't get turned on about what we are striving to be here at Global Markets, we both made a poor employment decision. We will help undo that mistake by making it real easy for you to go to work someplace else."

• • •

Magnetic service leadership is about leader making. When employees assume the leadership of their customer's experience in order to influence it, miracle making is possible. When employees experience the leadership responsibilities as a springboard for their ingenuity, miracle making is probable. Magnetic service leaders point the way, champion the way, and then get out of the way. They inspire far more than they inspect; they collaborate far more than they control.

Magnetic service leaders work hard to be the leader they wish to see in others. When employees feel stress, they model resilience and tenacity. When employees feel discouraged, they show goal-directed enthusiasm. And, when an employee feels affirmed by customers for a miracle received, magnetic service leaders honor the enchantment that employee has created by giving him or her all the credit. Magnetic service leaders have learned that the most important ingredient in the alchemy of miracle making is employee engagement that is enriched with a clear vision, a contagious spirit, and sincere gratitude.

• • •

"The bottom line is that leadership shows up in the inspired action of others."—Jack Weber

Chapter 13

Customers Are Empowered When Leaders Promote Partnerships

magnetism Magnetic force causes individual and random items to align in the direction of magnetic field.

magnetic service Magnetic service is steady. It leaves customers with a sense of power or security due to the fact that the varied and diverse units that customers must encounter are aligned and in sync in ways that are consistent and comfortable to customers.

It all started with a spark plug. A friend of ours reported that his weed eater refused to start on a springtime Saturday, and he surmised that the spark plug had given up the ghost. Mel drove to a nearby auto parts store for a replacement. The service counter person quickly determined that the plug Mel needed was not in stock at the store and that he'd have to call for one from their nearby warehouse.

"I need spark plug #232F ASAP!" the counter guy barked to the person who answered the warehouse phone. Mel sensed that he had suddenly been dropped in the middle of a battle zone. "Whaddaya mean you're on break? I'm your customer, goldarnnit, and I need some service right now!"

The counter guy hung up and tersely apologized to Mel for the wait. "Those warehouse people forget who they're working for," he snapped. "They don't give a darn that I'm the one out here on the firing line."

Mel told him to forget about it; he'd just take his rifle to another war zone down the street. "As I left," Mel said, "I heard him back on the phone to the poor soul in the warehouse. Their conversation was all about winning a feud, not about losing my funds."

If the employee of that auto parts company had known a little something about working in partnership with others, Mel would have walked away in a different frame of mind. He would have also been reassured that he, not the employee behind the counter, was the customer.

Internal Colleagues Are Not Internal Customers

It is popular nowadays to talk about internal and external customers. But this is a flawed concept. The attractiveness of the idea probably started with a line like, "If you're not serving the customer, you'd better be serving someone who is." It has a nice ring to it. But the clever line (from *Service America in the New Economy*) is about service, not about internal customership. To think otherwise would be the same as calling our significant other or our closest friends "customers." We try to be responsive to them or meet their needs, but we don't consider them to be customers.

Colleagues are partners, not customers. The difference between the two is great. The word "customer" implies confident deference;

partnerships are about equality. Serving customers suggests their needs take precedence over ours. That doesn't mean we engage in inappropriate or self-defeating actions. It means we become their servers, not their servants.

Let's go back to our spark plug story. The problem with the concept of an internal customer is two-fold. First, it creates a power struggle over who thinks who is in charge. Tons of wasted energy and precious time are spent pulling power plays and avoiding being put in a one-down position by another unit. None of us likes to be the "gofer" for anyone else.

The warehouse person probably made the counter guy the subject of his disparaging words to co-workers on his break. You can just hear him saying, "Those sales clerks think they run the place. They wouldn't last twenty minutes back here in this hot warehouse. They have no clue the amount of stuff we have to keep up with." And the next sales counter-to-warehouse interchange was probably even more dysfunctional. In such a situation, morale tumbles on both ends. Productivity is dragged down by ill will and subtle sabotage.

The other more insidious by-product of the "who's whose customer" war is the attention of both parties on internal conflict rather than on the real customer—the one writing the checks. The counter guy treated Mel like a kind of war correspondent—someone who was superfluous to the real battle. "As I left the store," Mel said later in amazement, "the clerk made no attempt to lasso me back into the fold. In fact, he seemed pleased that I took my funds elsewhere so he'd have another bullet in his blame gun to fire at the one he thought should be serving him."

Comfortable Processes Come from Competent Partnerships

A high-tech company had acquired a smaller software group to bolster their information technology capacity in providing more responsive sales support. The transition had been rocky, and six months after the acquisition, the CEO found himself snarling about the infighting going on between operations and sales. Customer complaints were climbing, field sales people were frustrated, and the new software enhancements the acquired company was supposed to produce were still stuck in applications development. Most grave was the fact that long-term loyal customers were threatening to walk.

"Why can't these folks quit arguing over who serves who and get busy thinking about how we all can serve the customer!" he snapped as he slammed his white-knuckled fist down on his oversized desk.

Teamwork and partnership are not the same things. Emulating the Dallas Cowboys or the Atlanta Falcons (Are we biased?!) *within* the operations department may heighten synergy and collective productivity. But it is the wrong model for the way in which the operations department should work with the sales department. An intact unit employs teamwork; between-unit synergy comes from partnership. Using teamwork tactics in a partnership context leads to flawed practices and counterproductive behavior. And it is, in fact, the inter-unit interaction that most frequently drives the quality of service processes.

Partnership thinking promotes inter-unit process improvement. Since the concept of power "over" does not exist in a partnership, units that both impact the customer are free to focus on how they can collaborate instead of compete.

A large health insurance provider in Boston received a great deal of customer complaints about the bureaucracy that was sometimes involved in processing a customer claim. The bottleneck came from two units—one that verified the medical aspects of the claim (what is the right fee for this procedure) and one that checked the legal and policy aspects of the claim (is this procedure covered under the policy). A long-running competition between the units over the resolution of grey areas that fell between them typically put some claims in the super-slow lane. When both unit leaders were replaced, the new leaders agreed to ignore history and work in partnership. Within a short time, no claim was taking longer than a few days to process. As the adage goes, "Great things can be accomplished when no one involved is concerned about who gets the credit."

Here are some of the takeaways for magnetic service leaders from each of these organizations.

Match Values, Not Just Talents

Partnerships can overcome a mismatch in capacities if the relationship springs from solidly congruent values. "We realized that we were 'two left feet' early on," said Frank Esposito, CEO of the global power-sport aftermarket distributor Tucker-Rocky Distributing, of his company's alliance with a Taiwan company working with Tucker-Rocky on a major helmet project. "But because we shared the same values of honesty, fair play, and commitment, we were able to shore up our mismatch before it derailed our effort."

Customers see a service provider as a single identity, even though they are often forced to deal with multiple units. They are unconcerned with organizational structure and resent reminders of who does or does not do what. If one unit with whom they must deal is customer-driven and another unit is not, the net impression of the customer migrates toward the negative.

When leaders promote partnership thinking, they foster the resolution of conflicting principles and colliding norms. Great partnerships share common values. Not only does cooperation emerge (augmenting the customer's sense of security), but valuable improvements in efficiency and productivity are made possible. With enhanced efficiency comes increased customer confidence, confidence that leaves a customer feeling empowered.

The high-tech CEO we described earlier asked each division head to write down four work values that his unit would refuse to concede in a conflict. When both divisions discovered that three of their four values were the same, they found new energy for collaboration and immediately set about working to accommodate the fourth value that was different. The more they came from their values, the more they came to view their differences as minor to petty.

Nurture Equality, Not Just Synergy

If partnerships are to be equality-based alliances, effort must be devoted to nurturing and bolstering that equality. The CEO's troubles with sales and operations were in part caused by their battles over turf, influence, and recognition. Operations did not want sales horning in on their territory; sales did not want operations getting the right to influence certain decisions that sales considered to be in their purview. Power *over* was the driver, not power *with*.

When the CEO later brought the two groups together for a meeting and reassured them that turf and influence were not relevant, and that recognition was not in jeopardy, they let go of their tug-of-war to decide "who was going to be in charge." "If our support staff at global headquarters thinks they have to lose their uniqueness in order to effectively partner with the regional staff in the field, they lose the fruitfulness of their diversity," says Steve Joyce, SVP of Strategic Alliances for Marriott International. "The reverse is equally true."

Value Early Warnings

Great partnerships work out cues that signal hiccups in the relationship. Such gestures become the preamble to candid confrontation that is aimed at getting the relationship back on track. Feedback is seen as nurturance (a kind of performance fertilizer) rather than critique.

A key question our high-tech CEO asked both sales and operations was this: "How much time elapses between when your gut tells you there's tension in the relationship and when your partner hears you talk about that tension?" When both divisions agreed to work toward a zero time lapse, assumptions were quickly clarified and innuendos were traded in for frankness.

Magnetic service starts by acknowledging that the real customer is the person who elevates your revenue, your membership, or your reputation. Colleagues are partners who retain their independence as you work interdependently to understand and meet your customers' needs.

Set collective goals that cause one unit's success to be dependent on another's support, and vice versa. Outline relationship agreements regarding communications, trust, and control. Talk to each other periodically about signs of power and signals of betrayal. Stop the power wars by together clarifying the identity of the real customer and outlining tangible goals to serve that customer.

Meet often to examine and eliminate barriers to giving great service to the ultimate customer. Collectively remain vigilant for the troublesome unit-to-unit junctures where silos are created and bureaucracies are spawned. Assert the truth when behavior or performance wavers from what you agreed to. Keep your promises or renegotiate them in good faith with ample lead time. Honor your partner by sharing credit and seeking ways to affirm one another's contributions. Keep your sights tenaciously on the partnership's purpose, not on turf.

. . .

Service involves working harmoniously as much with partners as with customers. To serve is to responsively assist. To serve is to generously support. It has nothing to do with power and everything to do with contribution. So, the adage, "If you're not serving the customer, your job is to be serving someone who is" might need some adjustment. "While you're serving the customer, your job is also to be serving others who are."

For customers, comfortable service involves getting what they want in a fashion that is seamless and anxiety-free, with no negative surprises. Service is magnetic when leaders are able to manage their organizational interminglings with the care they would give to a marriage rather than the discipline they would demand of a group of athletes.

. . .

"You can take great people, highly trained and motivated, and put them in a lousy system, and the system will win every time."—Geary Rummler

Chapter 14

Character Is Revealed If Leaders Have Soul

magnetism A magnet is the substance of a compass that enables the user to locate true North.

magnetic service Magnetic service is upright. It discloses to the customer that the service has substance, that it is grounded in a set of core values gallantly honored by the service provider.

Few Revolutionary War heroes capture the imagination of young students like General Francis Marion. Marion was physically unattractive, stood only five feet tall, and walked with a pronounced limp (the by-product of jumping out of a second story window to avoid capture). But he had two qualities that made him a major contributor to the defeat of England: his courage (which helped him secure the rank of colonel at an early age), and his ingenuity (which earned him the name "The Swamp Fox"). He was a man of substance. He had, in a word, soul.

The Swamp Fox's hotly pursued Marion's Brigade frequently embarrassed the British Redcoats by using bold tactics that completely altered the way battles were traditionally fought. The British soldiers proceeded with orderly precision and methodical planning; Marion pitched battles from trees and bushes. The British wore bright red uniforms; Marion's Brigade donned camouflage.

The Swamp Fox's hit-and-run methods typically caught the British army completely off guard. Creatively engineered guerrilla tactics enabled Marion's small, under-resourced unit to take on a well-supplied enemy who had many times more troops. In one decisive victory, Marion was outnumbered twenty to one, and his soldiers had only three bullets each and no artillery. It was guerrilla warfare at its finest. Magnetic service is like guerrilla warfare—unconventional, maverick, and out of the ordinary. It requires a leader like Francis Marion, with courage enough to take the road less traveled

Francis Marion Was Courageous

Magnetic service leaders are, like Francis Marion, courageous. Not the show-off, fearless kind of courageous, but rather the "I only regret I have but one life to lose for my country" kind. Their courage wells up from a devotion to duty rather than from desperation. Such courage is seen in leadership that has its source in a deep commitment to customers as well as an insatiable desire to serve.

Jimmy Crippen, owner and manager of Crippen's Country Inn and Restaurant in Blowing Rock, North Carolina, knows the power of bold, do-the-right-thing action. The popular restaurant is an old bed-and-breakfast-style home on a quiet street near downtown. It was a busy Friday night, in mid-October, a time when throngs of people descend upon the quaint town to enjoy the beauty of the fall colors. A group of twelve people from Atlanta arrived at the restaurant. One of them had made a reservation with Jimmy six weeks prior. Unfortunately, Jimmy had logged the reservation in his book for Saturday evening. The restaurant was packed.

"I am absolutely booked and can't possibly accommodate twelve people, much less at the same table," reported Jimmy. "But have your party go to the bar—drinks are on the house—while I work on a solution." Minutes later a crew of six waiters were hauling tables and chairs from the kitchen to the large front porch of the restaurant. Before they could finish their first drink, the hungry out-of-towners were escorted to a spot that proved to offer the best seats in the house. Jimmy personally waited on their every need. A potential disaster was transformed into an enchanting evening because a bold leader walked his talk.

Customers are devoted to organizations that serve with honor. Serving honorably ensures agility and focus. Energy can be totally directed at real, substantive work when no time is being wasted looking over a shoulder. Similarly, customers know they don't have to waste time double checking to make sure that what was promised was delivered, that what was expected in fact comes true. No one has to spend precious mental or emotional energy trying to decipher innuendo or suspicious actions, or weaseling around political minefields.

"Associates within Ritz-Carlton Hotels not only operate with absolute unwavering character," says John Dravinski, GM of the Ritz-Carlton Laguna Niguel, "they honor each other and insist others do, as well. Bottom line: People here enjoy being kind to each other." Environments with character make clean dealings easy. Working in a setting where honor is a virtue better enables employees to always look ahead toward exciting, compelling goals, not back and forth and behind.

Magnetic service leaders are willing to go against the tide. Most leaders today have been inundated with the many ways they can violate employee rights and infringe on the sanctity of good public relations. Just as they have been instructed in acting like leaders, they have been informed to think like lawyers. Many have learned to surrender to unrealistic pressures (under the banner of some cause) when their consciences instead scream for acting on principle. Too many leaders would rather lose sleep than lose face. Such timidity has bred a cautiousness about controversy that has spread beyond complex employee relations issues. The dearth of value-based decisions has left too many organizations with a character deficit.

Francis Marion Was Prepared

Francis Marion grew up in the wetlands near the coastal town of Georgetown, South Carolina. He spent his childhood learning the ways of the swamp. By the time his family moved in 1747 to a newer plantation when Francis was fifteen, he was an expert on the wild. The swamp life never left his heart. When he formed Marion's Brigade, he set up his headquarters deep in the swamp near the Pee Dee River. By the late 1780s, his men were prepared to attack the British. Their expertise with terrain that was strange to the British soldiers bolstered their courage to play David and Goliath.

Research tells us the number one thing people fear is to make a speech. Speech coaches tell us that the number one antidote to fear is preparation. Sure, there are foolhardy souls who willingly leap into unknown waters without the life jacket of preparation. But most leaders find that their courage is strengthened by preparation. Dancers rehearse, soldiers play war games, planners create what-if scenarios, and product makers use dry runs. Granted, everything cannot be pilot tested. But magnetic leaders, like General Francis Marion, do their homework. "It isn't the will to win that's important," says the famous and controversial Texas Tech basketball coach Bobby Knight. "Everyone has the will to win. What's important is the will to *prepare* to win."

Southern Ohio Medical Center in Portsmouth, Ohio, had a problem in 1998. Press Ganey, the J.D. Power of healthcare, had rated SOMC in the bottom quartile among all hospitals in customer satisfaction. CEO Randy Arnett and Medical Director Kendall Stewart sounded the charge: We must change our culture quickly. Their challenge was compounded by the fact that Portsmouth was rural, remote, and economically depressed, sometimes making it difficult to attract the best medical talent. The challenge would require broad-based preparation and persistence.

Southern Ohio Medical Center began a journey that included a system-wide study of tools and techniques that were needed to alter the perception of patients. Employees spent countless hours in classes learning the skills of customer service. Committees devised new ways to measure performance and celebrate steps along their journey. The intensive and persistent preparation paid off. In 2001, just four years later, Press Ganey rated them in the 99th percentile. Their performance on RN/LPN employee satisfaction was in the top four among hospitals in the nation. "Excellence," says HRD director Betsey Clagg, "shows up as stunning execution. But it's really about a solid vision, a thoughtful plan, and preparation—lots of unglamorous, late-at-night, behind-the-scenes preparation."

Francis Marion Had a Cause

A British officer was invited to visit Marion's swamp camp under a flag of truce. Marion offered his visitor a sweet potato baked on a campfire and served on a slab of pine bark. "Surely this cannot be your usual food," said the British officer. "Actually," replied General Marion, "because you are our visitor we are fortunate to have more than our usual amount." When the British officer returned to the British unit's headquarters in Georgetown, his colonel asked why he was so somber. "I have seen an American general and his officers, without pay, and almost without clothes, living on roots in the swamp; and all for liberty! What chances have we against such men?"

Your own cause can be a deep commitment to the product or service you provide to the marketplace. "You've gotta be able to see the beauty in a hamburger bun, " said Ray Kroc, founder of McDonalds. Debbi Fields, founder of Mrs. Fields Cookies, echoed the same theme: "I am not a businesswoman. I'm a cookie person." Advertising legend David Ogilvy directed one of his copywriters to "Make it immortal." Southwest Airlines president and chief operating officer Colleen Barrett says it this way: "We are not an airline with great customer service. We are a great customer service organization that happens to be in the airline business."

Your cause can also be a compelling commitment to the values that you wish to demonstrate to employees and customers. S. Truett Cathy, the coauthor (with Ken Blanchard) of *The Generosity Factor* and founder of Chick-fil-A®, the sixth largest fast-food chain in the United States, is a deeply religious person. Like 1924 Olympic gold medal runner Eric Liddel who refused to compete on the Sabbath (whose story was told in the Academy Award-winning movie *Chariots of Fire*) Truett elected to remain closed on Sunday. While competitors KFC,

McDonald's, Burger King, and the like serve customers seven days a week, Truett has gained favor in the marketplace for courageously remaining faithful to his cause.

"I like dealing with an organization whose leaders 'stand for something!'" was a frequent answer when a major research firm asked customers, "What do you like most about the organizations to whom you are most loyal?" Chick-fil-A, Southwest Airlines, USAA, and The Container Store were some of the companies that received high marks. Stand-for-something leaders weren't the loud, flamboyant, get-your-name-in-the-paper types. Instead, they were courageous leaders who were clear, focused, and unwavering in their commitment to stay their course and stand their ground.

Francis Marion Was Connected

Marion valued his men and saw them as his partners, not his subordinates. In most army units, the commanders lived much better than their troops did. This was not Marion's style. With his troops he slept on the ground, wrapped in a single blanket. Often they only had sweet potatoes to eat; sometimes they became sick from bad water in the swamp. He deliberated on tactics with his privates, not just his sergeants. Shared hardship served to galvanize the zeal of the brigade, which drew its bravery from Marion's spirit and example.

Leaders often are heard to say, "It's lonely at the top." Such statements reveal a perspective that leadership is a top-down, controlling activity rather than a partnership with colleagues. When Apollo 13 astronaut Jim Lovell was asked how he dealt with the stark terror of being in a space capsule facing almost certain destruction he said, "We had an important job to do, and we were never alone." Great leaders may be by themselves at times, but they are never alone.

Connected leaders do not view accessibility as a passive "my door is always open" gesture. Connected leaders are out in front, there when you need them, behind the scenes, and perpetually "wandering around." Wandering around is far different from ambling around. Connected leaders make deliberate and purposeful efforts to be on the scene to teach, model, reinforce, and affirm.

Great leaders communicate a service mentality. Captain Michael Abrashoff is the former captain of the USS Benfold, the ship the U.S. Navy acclaimed to be its best-run ship. "On my first day aboard, when the chow line formed for the traditional Sunday lunch on the deck of the ship, I went to the back of the chow line," says Captain Abrashoff. "It had been a tradition that all officers went to the front of the chow line and then sat together in a different area of the deck. After getting my meal, I sat with the enlisted personnel. It signified to every sailor on board that I was there to support them, not the other way around."

Francis Marion Valued Ingenuity, Not Convention

The single feat that won Marion the admiration of colleagues and enemies alike was the manner in which he turned every obstacle into an opportunity. His "find a better way" guerilla warfare tactics have been the inspiration of many elite military units, including the Army Special Forces (Green Berets), the Navy Seals and numerous Marine Commando units.

Magnetic service is born of employee ingenuity. Ingenuity is the blue-collar cousin of creativity. Ingenuity is inventive problem solving, not just blue-sky imagining. It is more than breakthrough innovation; it is "make it work" resourcefulness. Ingenuity is cultivated when leaders communicate goals as problems to be solved, not just hills to climb. It flourishes when leaders invite employees to think like owners, not like worker bees, and when they approach employee relationships as partnerships in which communication is candid and information is shared.

Ingenuity arises in a culture that values curiosity. It is found in places where leaders ask questions to learn, not to inspect or critique; where they show compassion, concern, and genuine interest.

Francis Marion Faced Danger as Duty

Leaders are not fearless beings who stoically snub their nose at terror. They are real-life human beings who face danger standing on legs of rubber. Danger makes them as queasy as it does young recruits posed for their first taste of battle. But great leaders lean into danger out of a strong sense of duty and responsibility. "Everyone has butterflies in their stomach," says selling guru and author Zig Ziglar. "The only difference between a pro and an amateur is: The pro has the butterflies in formation." Leaders act like pros because they feel accountable to those they serve.

Francis Marion was not a romantic in search of a hero's funeral. He was a realist who pondered his own mortality with the same uncertainty as the next guy. He hurt when he was wounded; he felt remorse when he wronged another. In *The Life of General Francis Marion*, authors Peter Horry and Mason Weems write, "The Tories murdered several prisoners in cold blood. They said that Lieutenant Marion, at the sight of such horrid scenes, appeared much shocked, and seeing among them a man who had often been entertained at his uncle's table, he flew to him for protection, and threw himself into his arms."

· · ·

Magnetic service leaders are real business leaders, a lot like Francis Marion. Day in, day out, they wear their souls on their sleeves, showing the stuff they are made of. Or as John Ellis, in his *Fast Company* article "Strategy," tells it:

> Here's what real business leaders do. They go out and rally the troops, plant the flag, and make a stand. They confront hostile audiences and they deal with the press. If the issue is confidence, they conduct themselves confidently. If the issue is trust, they make their company's business transparent. If the issue is character, they tell the truth. They do not shirk responsibility; they assume command. Because a fundamental ingredient of business success is leadership. And the granular stuff of leadership is courage, conviction, and character.

· · ·

"Those who stand for nothing fall for anything."
—Alexander Hamilton

Farewell

Ethics is not a component of customer service. Ethics is fundamentally what service is made of. To serve is to enter into a covenant with a customer that promises that worth will be exchanged for worth in a manner that is satisfactory to both. Covenants are implied agreements laced with an expectation of honesty, fairness, and reliability. The customer does not wish to be surprised when the value of what is received is less than what was expected, any more than the service provider wishes to be disappointed should the customer not live up to his or her promises to pay. Therefore, giving poor service is not only rude business manners, it is also unethical business practice.

People without firm ground sink. And people without an internal compass of what is true and pure get lost along the way. Magnetic service leaders always know "true North." Their self-confidence comes from their self-awareness. "If I lose my honor," Shakespeare has Anthony tell Octavia before the battle with Augustus, "I lose myself." Confucius wrote: "The superior man understands what is right; the inferior man understands what will sell."

Magnetic service leaders are grounded in complete, total, wall-to-wall, no-exceptions integrity. They stand on integrity; they are constructed of integrity, they reek of integrity. Integrity is the color they are painted; and true blue is a very bright blue, seen for miles around. Such leaders do not offer half-assed integrity—as Tom Peters says, "There is no such thing as a minor lapse of integrity." Their integrity is as uncompromising as that of Abe Lincoln, who walked miles to return a book. They show their nobility when they courageously turn their backs on shady deals or unscrupulous actions.

Noble organizations and leaders are by no means perfect. We all fall from grace from time to time. But temporary mistakes never deter magnetic service leaders from pursuing a proper path. Occasional, unintentional acts of indiscretion carry a lesson for improvement and a reminder that the noble always carry a heavy dose of humility and not a trace of arrogance.

We live in a time when the world of business is under scrutiny because of a few well-publicized violations of public confidence. These blights occurred not through some momentary lapse of honor, but through a pervasive abuse of power, an arrogant pursuit of greed that victimized innocent employees and a trusting marketplace, and a flagrant disregard for the fundamentals of private enterprise. It will take years to reclaim the loss of trust these incidents engendered. Perhaps the return of people's confidence can occur in part through a renewed commitment to the important covenant we call "service."

We selected the word "magnetic" to accompany "service" as the title of this book. The word "magnetic" comes from the Greek word meaning "the stone of Magnesia." Magnesia is one of four territories of Thessaly in Greece. In Greek mythology, Magnesia was a place that perfectly combined mountains and sea. It was the place chosen by the gods of Olympus for their summer vacations, their festivities, and their ceremonies. It was described as a site that always brought hope, happiness, and harmony. As such, it was deemed by writers such as Homer and Euripides as "the perfect or ideal place," having a magical draw and promising a compelling experience.

As we bid you farewell and bring this book to a close, we invite you to let your magnetic service bring hope, happiness, and harmony to those on the other end of the covenants you share.

Notes

1 Tennessee Squire Association story used with written permission from the fine folks at the Jack Daniel Distillery in Lynchburg, Tennessee.

5 "Remarkable takes originality, passion, guts . . ." Godin, *In Praise of the Purple Cow*, p. 76.

10 "The purpose of an organization . . ." Drucker, *The Practice of Management*, p. 39.

17 Appreciation to Ron Zemke for his groundbreaking work on trust. Zemke's research has found there are five elements of trust: credibility, personal communications, task communications, fairness, and inclusion.

34 "Boards of Customers" . . . May 1991 Interview with Sharon A. Decker, former VP of customer service for Duke Energy, Charlotte, North Carolina.

38 Direct Connect motto used with permission from Fred Givhan, President of Direct Connect in Dallas, Texas.

40 "There is an energy field . . ." May, *Love and Will*, p. 312.

43 "Chip and his wife, Nancy were . . ." A version of this example appeared in *Customer Love: Attracting and Keeping Customers For Life*.

56 Asian girl's story from an October 2002 interview with Kitty Scott, director of patient relations at The Children's Hospital of Boston.

76 Desmond, "Intuit Online," p. 152. The Southern Pipe and Supply example first appeared in *Beep Beep! Competing in the Age of the Roadrunner* by Bell and Harari.

79 "Researcher Arie de Geus found that . . ." de Geus, *The Living Company*, p. 9.

91 "Our goal is not . . ." Alan Shaffer quote from Bell and Harari, *Beep Beep!*, p. 43.

98 "Those people . . . "Napoleon Barragan quote from Zemke, "Can You Manage Trust?", p. 76.

100 "One of the surest signs . . ." Levitt, "After the Sale is Over . . .", p. 88.

102 "Keeping Agreement . . ." Hendricks and Ludeman, *The Corporate Mystic*, p. 45.

111 "Boldness has genius . . ." Murray, *Scottish Himalayan Expedition*, p. 206.

115 "A lot of us think . . ." Koehn quote from Hammonds, "No Risk, No Reward," p. 92.

122 "I had parents who gave me . . ." Rice quote from Reed, "The President's Prodigy," p. 398.

128 "The first responsibility of a leader . . ." DePree, *Leadership is an Art*, p. 9.

130 John R. Patterson is currently President of Progressive Insights, Inc., in Atlanta.

135 "If you're not serving . . ." Zemke and Albrecht, *Service America in the New Economy*, p. 153.

143 "Associates within Ritz-Carlton Hotels . . . ." Dravinski, quote originally appeared in *Beep Beep!* p. 136.

145 Story about Marion's swamp camp from Cornelius, *Francis Marion: The Swamp Fox*, p. 49.

148 "The Tories murdered several . . ." Horry and Weems, *The Life of General Francis Marion*, p 131.

148 "Here's what real business leaders . . .." Ellis, "Strategy," p. 74.

References

Bell, Bilijack R. and Chip R. Bell, "Building a Cult-Like Following," *Realtor Magazine*, August 2002.

Bell, Chip R., *Customer Love: Attracting and Keeping Customers For Life*, Provo, UT: Executive Excellence Publishing, 2000.

Bell, Chip R., *Customers As Partners: Building Relationships That Last,* San Francisco: Berrett-Koehler Publishers, Inc., 1994.

Bell, Chip R. and Bilijack R. Bell, *Bold Leaders Inspire Magnetic Service,* Executive Excellence Publishing, August 2003.

Bell, Chip R. and Bilijack R. Bell, "Staffing Stunning People for Stunning Service," *Staff Digest*, July-August 2002.

Bell, Chip and Oren Harari, *Beep Beep! Competing in the Age of the Road Runner*, New York: Warner Books, 2000.

Bell, Chip R. and Heather Shea (Schultz), *Dance Lessons: Six Steps to Great Partnerships in Business and Life*, San Francisco: Berrett-Koehler Publishers, Inc., 1998.

Bell, Chip R. and Ron Zemke, *Managing Knock Your Socks Off Service*, New York: AMACOM Books, 1992.

Berry, Leonard L., *Discovering the Soul of Service*, New York: The Free Press, 1999.

Blanchard, Kenneth and Sheldon Bowles, *Raving Fans,* New York: William Morrow and Company, 1993.

Blanchard, Ken and S. Truett Cathy, *The Generosity Factor,* New York: Zondervan, 2002.

Burns, Tom and George Stalker, *The Management of Innovation,* London: Tavistock Publications, 1961.

Connellan, Thomas K. *Bringing Out the Best in Others: Three Keys for Business Leaders, Educators, Coaches and Parents.* Austin, TX: Bard Press, 2003.

Connellan, Tom, *Inside the Magic Kingdom.* Austin, TX: Bard Press, 1996.

Cornelius, Kay, *Francis Marion: The Swamp Fox*, Philadelphia: Chelsea House, 2001.

DePree, Max, *Leadership is an Art,* New York: Doubleday, 1989.

Desmond, Edward W., "Intuit Online," *Fortune,* April 13, 1998, pp. 149-152.

Dow, Roger and Sue Cook, *Turned On!* New York: HarperCollins, 1996.

Drucker, Peter F., *The Practice of Management*, New York: Harper & Row, 1954.

Ellis, John, "Strategy," *Fast Company*, October 2002, p. 74.

Felix, Antonia, *Condi: The Condoleezza Rice Story*, New York: Newmarket Press, 2002.

Forster, Edward Morgan, *Howard's End,* New York: Knopf, 1910.

Godin, Seth, "In Praise of the Purple Cow," *Fast Company,* February, 2003, pp. 74–79.

Godin, Seth, *Purple Cow: Transform Your Business by Becoming Remarkable.* Boston: Do You Zoom, 2003. Available only through www.apurplecow.com.

Godin, Seth, *Permission Marketing: Turning Strangers into Friends, and Friends into Customers*, New York: Simon & Schuster, 1999.

Griffin, Jill, *Customer Loyalty: How to Earn It, How to Keep It*, New York: The Free Press, 1995.

Hammonds, Keith, "No Risk, No Reward," *Fast Company*, April 2002, pp. 82-93.

Harari, Oren, *Leapfrogging the Competition: Five Giant Steps to Market Leadership*, Washington, D. C.: American Century Press, 1997.

Harari, Oren, *The Leadership Secrets of Colin Powell*, New York: McGraw-Hill, 2002.

Heil, Gary, Tom Parker and Deborah C. Stephens, *One Size Fits One*, New York: John Wiley, 1997.

Hendricks, Gay and Kate Ludeman, *The Corporate Mystic*, New York: Bantam, 1996.

Hill, Sam and Glenn Rifkin, *Radical Marketing*, New York: HarperBusiness, 1999.

Horry, Peter and Mason Weems, *The Life of General Francis Marion*, Winston-Salem, NC: John F. Blair, 2000.

Keiningham, Timothy and Terry Vavra, *The Customer Delight Principle*, New York: McGraw-Hill, 2001.

Levinson, Jay Conrad and Seth Godin, *The Guerilla Marketing Handbook,* Boston: Houghton Mifflin Company, 1994.

Levitt, Theodore, "After the Sale Is Over . . .", *Harvard Business Review*, September-October 1983, pp. 88-94.

Lundin, Stephen C., Harry Paul, and John Christensen. *Fish! A Remarkable Way to Boost Morale and Improve Results*. New York: Hyperion, 2000.

Matthews, Peter (ed.), *The Guinness Book of Records 1994*, New York: Guinness Publishing Ltd., 1993.

May, Rollo, *Love and Will,* New York: Dell, 1969.

MacKenzie, Gordon, *Orbiting the Giant Hairball,* New York: Viking, 1998.

McNally, David and Karl D. Speak, *Be Your Own Brand*. San Francisco: Berrett-Koehler, 2002.

Morris, Desmond, *The Naked Ape: A Zoologist's Study of the Human Animal,* New York: Delta, 1987.

Naylor, Mary and Susan Greco, *Customer Chemistry*, New York: McGraw-Hill, 2002.

Newell, Frederick, *Loyalty.Com*, New York: McGraw-Hill, 2000.

O'Dell, Susan M. and Joan A. Pajunen, *The Butterfly Customer: Capturing the Loyalty of Today's Elusive Consumer*, Toronto: John Wiley & Sons Canada, 1997.

Peppers, Don and Martha Rogers, *The One to One Manager: Real-World Lessons in Customer Relationships,* New York, Doubleday, 1999.

Peters, Tom and Robert Waterman, *In Search of Excellence*, New York: Harper & Row, 1982.

Peterson, Robert, "Measuring Customer Satisfaction: Fact or Artifact," University of Texas Working Paper, quoted in Ron Zemke, "What's Love Got To Do With It," *The Service Edge Newsletter*, January 1991, p. 8.

Pine, Joseph and James Gilmore, *The Experience Economy*, Boston: Harvard Business School Press, 1999.

Ragas, Matthew and Bolivar Bueno, *The Power of Cult Branding*, Roseville, CA: Prima Venture, 2002.

Reed, Julia, "The President's Prodigy," *Vogue,* Vol. 191, No. 10, pp. 396–403, 448–449.

Reichheld, Frederick, *The Loyalty Effect,* Boston: Harvard Business School Press, 1996.

Reichheld, Frederick, *Loyalty Rules! How Today's Leaders Build Lasting Relationships*, Boston: Harvard Business School Press, 2001.

Rosen, Emanuel, *The Anatomy of Buzz*, New York: Doubleday, 2000.

Sanders, Betsy, *Fabled Service*, San Francisco: Jossey-Bass, 1995.

Sewell, Carl and Paul B. Brown, *Customers For Life: How To Turn That One-Time Buyer into a Lifetime Customer*, New York: Doubleday, 1990.

Spoelstra, Jon, *Marketing Outrageously*, Austin: Bard Press, 2001.

Teerlink, Rich and Lee Ozley, *More Than a Motorcycle: The Leadership Journey at Harley-Davidson*, Boston: Harvard Business School Press, 2000.

Travis, Daryl, *Emotional Branding*, Roseville, CA: Prima Venture, 2000.

Wiersema, Fred, *Customer Intimacy*, Santa Monica, CA: Knowledge Exchange, 1996.

Zemke, Ron, "Can You Manage Trust?" *Training Magazine*, February 2000. pp. 76-85.

Zemke, Ron and Chip R. Bell, *Service Magic: How to Amaze Your Customers*, Chicago: Dearborn Trade, 2003.

Zemke, Ron and Chip R. Bell, *Knock Your Socks Off Service Recovery*, New York: AMACOM Books, 2000.

Zemke, Ron and Karl Albrecht, *Service America in the New Economy*, New York: McGraw-Hill, 2002.

Zemke, Ron and Tom Connellan, *E-Service*, New York: AMACOM Books, 2001.

Thanks!

The only solitary thing about a book is reading it. Everything else is a collective effort—especially taking it from idea to inventory. We have far more people to thank than space will allow and memory can recall.

The unsung contributors to this book are the many inspiring, influential people whose philosophy and practices are the exemplars of what this book is about. How do you thank the nameless hotel housekeeper who found you an electrical adapter for your laptop without being asked? Or the airport shoeshine man who trusted you to come back and pay him when he couldn't break your twenty? Or the taxi driver who refused to accept a hefty taxi fare because a sudden unavoidable stop resulted in coffee spilled on your flight bag? They—and countless like them—remind us of the innate goodness of most of humanity and the important need for more magnetic service.

There are people we can name, though, who played a role in shepherding this work on our behalf. Our clients gave us powerful insights and told us poignant incidents, many of which we wove into the text. We owe much to our work partners—particularly Ron Zemke, Tom Connellan, and Jill Applegate at Performance Research Associates in Minneapolis and Orlando, as well as Bruce Wilson, Charlie Hull, Watt Neal, Rusty Epperson, Rick Spiller, Furman Wood, Joseph Rogers, and Charles Hardin at Wilson, Hull & Neal in Atlanta. All of these helpers provided their own brand of encouragement and assistance.

The book-making crew was led by Steve Piersanti, president of Berrett-Koehler Publishers in San Francisco. Unlike most publishing company presidents, Steve played a vital and active role in helping us shape the concepts and sharpen our communication. Through many e-mails and conference calls, he nudged us to plumb the depths of our knowledge in order to make this the best book it could be. We are grateful for his commitment, his candor, and his collaboration. The many people of the Berrett-Koehler team were always there for us with enthusiasm and professionalism.

We owe a debt of gratitude to the reviewers who carefully read the first draft and provided excellent and insightful feedback: Kathleen Epperson, Susan Anthony, Sara Jane Hope, Ariel Jolicoeur, and Frank Basler.

Leslie Stephen in Austin, Texas, was our world-class editor. She brought her extraordinary talent to bear on our rough scribblings and partially baked ideas, honing them into understandable prose that made us very proud. She was always there for us—day and night—providing awesome turnaround and work of remarkable clarity and quality. We also benefited from the meticulous editing work of Marguerite Rigoglioso, who greatly improved the readability of the book.

We are deeply grateful for the love and affection of our extended family, who frequently queried us with "How's the book coming?" Writing a book together was a wonderful refresher in the importance of family. Rivers Bell in Atlanta and Padre Bell in Dallas reminded us daily that the principal component of encouragement is unconditional acceptance.

•   •   •

Finally, we thank our wives—Nancy and Lisa—to whom this book is dedicated. They provided living examples of passionate devotion. Without their tireless support, infectious enthusiasm, and abiding love, this book would not have been possible.

To all of you, our humble, heartfelt "thank you."

Thanks!

Index

Index

Index

Index

Index

Index

Index

About the Authors

Chip R. Bell

Chip R. Bell is a senior partner with Performance Research Associates, Inc., and manages their Dallas, Texas office. His consulting practice focuses on helping organizations to build a culture that supports long-term customer devotion. Prior to starting a consulting firm in the late 1970s, he was director of management and organization development for NCNB, now Bank of America.

Chip is the author or co-author of fifteen books, including *Service Magic: How to Amaze Your Customers* (with Ron Zemke); *Customer Love: Attracting and Keeping Customers for Life*; *Customers As Partners: Building Relationships That Last*; *Managers As Mentors: Building Partnerships For Learning*; *Managing Knock Your Socks Off Service* (with Ron Zemke); *Dance Lessons: Six Steps to Great Partnerships in Business and Life* (with Heather Shea); and *Beep-Beep!: Competing in the Age of the Road Runner* (with Oren Harari). His work has been featured on CNBC, CNN, Bloomberg TV, NPR, Voice of America, and Reuters and in the *Wall Street Journal; Fortune; USA Today; Entrepreneur Magazine; Inc. Magazine; Business Week;* and *Bottom Line Business.*

Chip has served as a consultant, keynote speaker, or trainer to such major organizations as IBM, Microsoft, General Electric, Royal Bank, Marriott, Pfizer, Sears, Merrill Lynch, Ritz-Carlton, 3M, USAA, Aurora Health, Lockheed-Martin, Harley-Davidson, Honda, MBNA, Bank of

America, Universal Studios, Pepsi, AAA, Duke Energy, and Victoria's Secret. He was a highly decorated infantry unit commander with the elite 82nd Airborne in Vietnam. Chip is married to Nancy Rainey Bell, a school administrator and attorney.

Bilijack R. Bell

Bilijack R. Bell is a commercial real estate professional with Wilson, Hull & Neal in Atlanta. With eight years in commercial real estate, he has a solid reputation for highly creative approaches to client service. That reputation has earned him membership in both the prestigious President's Club as well as the Million Dollar Club. His service articles have appeared in such publications as *Realtor Magazine*, *Staff Digest*, *Executive Excellence*, and *Midas Matters*.

Bilijack is a graduate of Elon College in Burlington, North Carolina, where he majored in history. He was a member of the 1989 U.S. Ambassador Soccer team and competed throughout Europe. Bilijack is married to Lisa Dickinson Bell, a middle school teacher in the Atlanta area.

For information on keynotes, workshops, training programs and other *Magnetic Service* resources, log on to *www.magneticservice.com*.

. . .

Want to send someone a sample of this book? We post a chapter a month on our Web site. You can also download the PDF file for your personal use. Send us your favorite magnetic service story. We give away a free book each month to the person who submits the best story.

. . .

Chip R. Bell
25 Highland Park #100
Dallas, Texas 75205
214/522-5777
214/691-7591 (fax)
chip@chipbell.com
www.chipbell.com and *www.magneticservice.com*

. . .

Bilijack R. Bell
Wilson, Hull & Neal
1600 Northside Drive, NW
Atlanta, Georgia 30318
404/352-1882
404/351-2701 (fax)
bbell@whnre.com
www.whnre.com and *www.magneticservice.com*

Berrett-Koehler Publishers

Berrett-Koehler is an independent publisher of books and other publications at the leading edge of new thinking and innovative practice on work, business, management, leadership, stewardship, career development, human resources, entrepreneurship, and global sustainability.

Since the company's founding in 1992, we have been committed to creating a world that works for all by publishing books that help us to integrate our values with our work and work lives, and to create more humane and effective organizations.

We have chosen to focus on the areas of work, business, and organizations, because these are central elements in many people's lives today. Furthermore, the work world is going through tumultuous changes, from the decline of job security to the rise of new structures for organizing people and work. We believe that change is needed at all levels—individual, organizational, community, and global—and our publications address each of these levels.

To find out about our new books,
special offers,
free excerpts,
and much more,
subscribe to our free monthly eNewsletter at

www.bkconnection.com

Please see next pages for other books
from Berrett-Koehler Publishers

Customers As Partners
Building Relationships That Last

Chip R. Bell

Written with passion and humor, this ground-breaking work provides step-by-step guidelines for enhancing long-term customer loyalty and achieving lasting success. Chip Bell offers insights on how to keep the quality of customer relationships central in every interaction by creating sustaining personal bonds—the true source of a company's profitability.

Paperback, 256 pages • ISBN 1-881052-78-8 • Item #52788-415 $15.95

Hardcover • ISBN 1-881052-54-0 • Item #52540-415 $24.95

Dance Lessons
Six Steps to Great Partnerships in Business and Life

Chip R. Bell and Heather Shea

Dance Lessons is a comprehensive guide to the interpersonal side of partnerships, revealing exactly how the champions choreograph their partnership dances for show-stopping performances. Bell and Shea offer an in-depth look at how we can successfully manage partnerships and build them with substance—passion, quality, heart, and soul—and show how to develop meaningful, ethical, and soulful partnerships in every interaction in your work and your life.

Hardcover, 200 pages • ISBN 1-57675-043-4 • Item #50434-415 $24.95

Audiotape, 2 cassettes/3 hours • ISBN 1-5651-1272-5
Item #12725-415 $17.95

Managers As Mentors
Building Partnerships for Learning

Chip R. Bell

Managers As Mentors is a provocative guide to helping associates grow and adapt in today's tumultuous organizations. Chip Bell persuasively shows that today, mentoring means valuing creativity over control, fostering growth by facilitating learning, and helping others get smart, not just get ahead. His hands-on, down-to-earth advice takes the mystery out of effective mentoring, teaching leaders to be the confident coaches integral to learning organizations.

Paperback, 206 pages • ISBN 1-57675-034-5 • Item #50345-415 $16.95

Berrett-Koehler Publishers
PO Box 565, Williston, VT 05495-9900
Call toll-free! **800-929-2929** 7 am–9 pm Eastern Standard Time

Or fax your order to 802-864-7627
For fastest service order online: **www.bkconnection.com**

Attracting Perfect Customers
The Power of Strategic Synchronicity

Stacey Hall and Jan Brogniez

Go beyond guerrilla marketing, relationship selling, and permission marketing to a place where there is an abundance of perfect customers and clients just waiting to be served. The authors lead readers step-by-step through a paradigm shift in their approach to sales and marketing. Readers will learn to use the Strategic Attraction Planning™ process, which requires just five minutes of planning each day and makes businesses so highly attractive that perfect customers and clients are drawn to them, like a lighthouse in a storm.

Paperback, 200 pages • ISBN 1-57675-124-4 • Item #51244-415 $17.95

The Referral of a Lifetime
The Networking System
That Produces Bottom-Line Results... Every Day!

Tim Templeton

Part of The Ken Blanchard Series, *The Referral of a Lifetime* teaches a step-by-step system that will allow anyone to generate a steady stream of new business through consistent referrals from existing customers and friends and, at the same time, maximize business with existing customers.

Hardcover, 144 pages • 1-57675-240-2 • Item #52402-415 $19.95

301 Ways to Have Fun at Work

Dave Hemsath and Leslie Yerkes
Illustrated by Dan McQuillen

In this entertaining and comprehensive guide, Hemsath and Yerkes show readers how to have fun at work—everyday. Written for anyone who works in any type of organization, *301 Ways to Have Fun at Work* provides more than 300 ideas for creating a dynamic, fun-filled work environment.

Paperback, 300 pages • ISBN 1-57675-019-1 • Item #50191-415 $14.95

Berrett-Koehler Publishers
PO Box 565, Williston, VT 05495-9900
Call toll-free! **800-929-2929** 7 am-9 pm Eastern Standard Time
Or fax your order to 802-864-7627
For fastest service order online: **www.bkconnection.com**